Grammar
and
Composition

BY CAROLYN KANE

COPYRIGHT © 2011 Mark Twain Media, Inc.

ISBN 978-1-58037-569-6

Printing No. CD–404156

Mark Twain Media, Inc., Publishers
Distributed by Carson-Dellosa Publishing LLC

Visit us at www.carsondellosa.com

TABLE OF CONTENTS

FOREWORD TO THE TEACHER

This activity book is an overview of English grammar and an introduction to the basic elements of composition. The book begins with the simplest grammatical elements—words—and proceeds through sentences, paragraphs, and the complete composition. The concern here is for the fundamentals of the English language rather than the myriad details and exceptions that are best left for study beyond junior high school.

Throughout the work, I have stressed that grammar is a study of the *structure* of language, not a list of "rules" to be memorized and obeyed. I have also used examples to illustrate how the study of grammar can be a useful pursuit for anyone who wants or needs to be a good writer. Finally, I have tried to give some indication of the satisfaction and pleasure that come from writing a well-constructed sentence, paragraph, or essay. Each writer in a classroom will develop grammar and composition skills at their own pace. The chapters in this book are arranged from easiest to most challenging, allowing each student to master the lessons before moving on. This is helpful for students who move at a slower pace or need individualized instruction.

Wherever possible, the assignments give students writing prompts so they can develop sentences or short compositions of their own, rather than analyze sentences that I have written. This approach should give students a chance to practice what they have learned and help them to retain information. Exciting topics are designed to make the activities feel less like assignments and more like self-sponsored writing. Critical thinking questions encourage students to analyze the readings and write about what they think is happening or will happen next. Other activities feature short answer, constructed response questions.

Although the chapters are short, it would be inadvisable for a student to work through more than one chapter in any given day, because the vocabulary of grammar is difficult for some students to master. Grammar is best studied slowly, in small doses. Each chapter includes a "Writing Tip" to make it easier for students to remember rules or to provide additional information. Much like developing a working vocabulary through reading challenging texts instead of memorizing word lists, correct grammar usage is best reinforced through writing and rewriting. Mistakes are a natural part of learning any new skill. By providing guidance instead of punishment for each grammar and composition skill, you can provide your students with the writing skill set to take them from your classroom to high school, college, and beyond.

I am indebted to Dr. Claude Faulker, who for many years was the Chairman of the English Department at the University of Arkansas. As a student in his college-level course, I found his approach to be highly useful in developing my own prose style, and in writing this book, I have tried to adapt some of his methods for the use of students in secondary schools.

This book is dedicated to Linda Buechting, in appreciation for her talent as a writer and in gratitude for years of support and encouragement.

—THE AUTHOR

1

INTRODUCTION

Getting in Practice

Writing is fun. What could be more satisfying than to fill a blank page with words that will make people shake with laughter, brush away tears, boil over with anger, sit up and pay attention, or race to the polls to cast a vote? What could be more fulfilling than to create sentences, poems, ideas, emotions, people, and places out of nothing but one's own mind? What can make the spirit soar like signing autographs or hearing a friend say, "Hey, I read your story in the newspaper last night!"?

Think of the many people who write for a living or who do some kind of work that involves writing. First, or course, there are professional writers: novelists, poets, journalists, script writers, playwrights, people who write books of advice, and people who write stories and articles for magazines. Then there are people who teach others how to write in grade schools, high schools, and colleges. Lawyers, teachers, doctors, and other professionals are often required to write articles as part of their jobs. Someone has to write advertisements for the businesses of our country, and somebody has to edit all of the newspapers and magazines that we read every day. Somebody has to write instruction manuals, and someone even has to write the textbooks for school (although sometimes we might wish that the textbook writers would take a long vacation). Not every writer lives in Hollywood or New York; writers are all around us.

Like any skill, good writing requires practice. A pianist must learn his key signatures and play a great many scales and keyboard exercises before he can step into the spotlight to play Beethoven's "Emperor" Concerto with the Chicago Symphony Orchestra. A football player has to train long hours before he can perfect his breathtaking forward pass or make a 60-yard touchdown run that will bring the cheering crowd to its feet. Likewise, before a writer can begin serious work on a best-selling novel or the article that will win the Pulitzer Prize, he or she has to know the writer's building blocks and tools: nouns, verbs, modifiers, phrases, clauses, commas, semicolons, colons, dashes, and parentheses. A person who makes a serious study of such matters is called a **grammarian** or a **linguist**. The study of language is called **grammar.**

This book is designed to get a young writer "in practice," so to speak, and to train the writer's hand and brain for useful and satisfying work. As you read the chapters and work the exercises, remember the old saying: "Practice makes perfect!"

> **Writing Tip:** The more you write, the better your writing becomes, so keep writing!

Name: _Jazz-1_____ Date: _____

ASSIGNMENT: Writing in Everyday Life

1. Do you know anyone who does a lot of writing as part of his or her job? Who?

   Yes my mom writes a lot for her Job.

2. Do you have any ideas about what you want to be when you grow up? What are some of the possibilities?

   I want to be a horse trainer, stable owner, or a horse camp owner.

3. Do any of these careers involve writing? If so, how?

   Yes I would have to write down

4. What sorts of writing projects are you required to do as part of your schoolwork?

   _____

   _____

   _____

5. Have you ever read anything that was badly written? If so, how could it have been improved?

   _____

   _____

   _____

6. If you were a professional writer, what kind of work would you like to do? (Sports writing? Television scripts? Novels?)

   _____

   _____

   _____

PART ONE: WORDS

1. Nouns

Words are the basic units of composition. A writer builds sentences from words, paragraphs from sentences, and a whole composition from paragraphs—anything from a one-page essay to a thousand-page book. In order to write well, a student must learn to recognize the different types of words and how to use them.

A **noun** is a word that names a person, place, or thing. Such nouns as *cat, book, family, river, doctor, school, town,* and *pencil* are familiar words to all of us. A noun might also name an idea, a concept, or a personality trait, as in *courage, honesty, anger, friendship, time, eternity,* and *hope.*

Nouns come in several types. A **common noun** is the name of a general type of person, place, or thing: examples are *dog, lawyer, vampire, lake, city, school,* and *street.* A **proper noun** names a particular person or a specific thing: *Lassie, Perry Mason, Count Dracula, Lake Michigan, Chicago, Harvard University, Kennedy Boulevard.* (Notice that in a proper noun, the first letter of each word is capitalized.) Nouns also come in **singular** and **plural** varieties. A singular noun names only one person or thing; a plural noun names two or more. Most nouns form the plural by adding the letter "s" or the letters "es": one *tree,* several *trees;* one *box,* several *boxes.* But a few nouns form their plurals in odd ways: one *child,* several *children;* one *mouse,* several *mice;* one *deer,* a herd of *deer.* A **collective** noun is the name of a group: *team, orchestra, choir, committee, jury, class.*

It is important to understand the difference between **concrete** and **abstract** nouns. A concrete noun is the name of something that can be seen, heard, touched, tasted, or smelled. Examples are *hamburger, trumpet, velvet, sandpaper,* and *floor.* An abstract noun is the name of an idea or concept that cannot be perceived with the senses: *happiness, freedom, excellence, failure, gloom, perversity, irritation.* Nouns come in different degrees of abstraction. The word *animal* is highly abstract: an animal can be anything from an amoeba to a whale. The word *dog* is somewhat more concrete but difficult to picture; there is a big difference between a St. Bernard and a Chihuahua. But if I write that Lassie is a *collie,* a reader has a good idea of the size and shape of her body, the color and texture of her fur, and the depth of her bark. My reader can see Lassie in his mind's eye.

Readers love to form pictures in their minds, and they enjoy imagining sights, sounds, textures, and smells. Abstract nouns like *truth* and *bravery* are valuable, but if you use too many such words, your compositions will lack excitement and imagination. In particular, beware of nouns so abstract that they mean almost nothing: *case, factor, feature, subject, situation, instance.* Use these words only when you can't possibly think of anything else. Also beware of abstract slang nouns like *hassle* and *stuff.* Let your language be as specific as possible.

Writing Tip: Use as many concrete nouns as possible.

Name: _____ Date: _____

ASSIGNMENT: Working with Nouns

1. Rewrite each of the following common nouns as a proper noun.

   Example: river—Mississippi River

   politician _____

   mountain _____

   athlete _____

   town _____

   team _____

2. Rewrite each abstract noun as a more concrete noun:

   toy _____

   game _____

   worker _____

   tool _____

   monster _____

3. Clip a short article from a newspaper or magazine and circle every noun. Which are the common nouns and which are proper? Can you tell the difference between singular, plural, and collective nouns?

   _____

   _____

   _____

4. Write a description of your home, your neighborhood, or some other place you visit often. Use as many concrete nouns as possible and at least two proper nouns.

   _____

   _____

   _____

PART ONE: WORDS

2. Pronouns

A **pronoun** is a word that takes the place of a noun. (In this case, "pro" means "substituting for" or "acting as"; hence the name "pronoun.") A few common pronouns are *he, them, mine, this, those, none, everyone,* and *myself.* Without pronouns, both writing and reading would be a difficult and tedious business. Imagine trying to tell a story if you could never substitute a pronoun for a noun:

> *Joe listened intently for sounds in the hall. Hearing no sounds in the hall, Joe tiptoed out of Joe's room, slipped through the back door, sprang on Joe's bicycle, and pedaled as fast as Joe could. Joe had to find Kristin in time to warn Kristin about the mysterious flickering lights in the old Grizzard mansion. Joe would never have believed in the lights if Joe had not seen the lights with Joe's own eyes. Now Joe could have kicked Joe for not finding Kristin and warning Kristin sooner.*

A smart reader can understand what is happening: Joe has apparently seen a ghost—or some kind of alien creature—and is afraid for the safety of his friend Kristin. But it is difficult to work up any good chills and shivers or to get worried about Joe and Kristin, because slogging through all those nouns is like wading through thick mud. Pronouns would make the story easier to read:

> *Joe listened intently for sounds in the hall. Hearing none, he tiptoed out of his room, slipped through the back door, sprang on his bicycle, and pedaled as fast as he could. He had to find Kristin in time to warn her about the mysterious flickering lights in the old Grizzard mansion. Joe would never have believed in those lights if he had not seen them with his own eyes. Now he could have kicked himself for not finding Kristin and warning her sooner.*

Like nouns, pronouns come in several types. Probably the ones we use most often are the **personal pronouns,** which refer to specific people and sometimes to things. In the passage above, *he* refers to Joe, *she* refers to Kristin, and *them* refers to the mysterious lights. Like nouns, personal pronouns come in singular and plural varieties. Unlike nouns, they change to show **first person** (the one speaking), **second person** (the one spoken to), and **third person** (the one spoken about). *He, she,* and *them* are all third-person pronouns.

> **Writing Tip:** Personal pronouns make your writing easier to read.

Here is a chart showing the different forms of personal pronouns:

	SINGULAR	**PLURAL**
First person	I, me, my, mine	we, us, our, ours
Second person	you, your, yours	you, your, yours
Third person	he, she, it him, her, his, hers, its	they, them, their, theirs

Other useful words are **demonstrative pronouns,** which point things out. There are only four such words in the English language: *this, that, these,* and *those,* as in "That is my desk, and those are my books."

Indefinite pronouns are vague: they refer to unknown people or things, or to no one in particular. Some examples are *anybody, anyone, everyone, everybody, someone, somebody, no one, nobody, something, both, few, many, none,* and *all.*

Reflexive pronouns end in *-self,* as in *Joe could have kicked himself,* or *I am furious with myself,* or *You should be proud of yourself.* These words can also be used as **intensive pronouns** to add emphasis, as in *Joe himself saw the ghost* or *Kristin herself was in great danger.*

Name: _____ Date: _____

ASSIGNMENT: Working with Pronouns

1. Circle the pronouns in the following passage:

Joe ran into the gymnasium and found it empty. "Kristin! Coach Wilson!" he shouted. "Miss Peterson! Anybody! Can you hear me?" But no one answered. Joe's shout echoed eerily among the shadows of the gymnasium. He looked in the locker room; it was also empty, and the door to Coach Wilson's office was locked. Apparently everyone had left for the day. "This is spooky," Joe said aloud. He always felt braver when he talked to himself.

Joe whistled to keep his courage strong as he tried to think of a plan. Then he remembered: sometimes Kristin went to the library to read, so maybe Joe would find her there. "That's a good idea," he said as he hurried back to the parking lot. "Next stop—the public library!" Suddenly he stopped and stared in disbelief. His bicycle was gone! Someone, or something, had taken it. "*Now* what do I do?" he said in a shaking voice. He could never reach the library on foot—not before sunset. Sherlock Holmes himself couldn't find a way out of such a mess.

2. Write sentences containing the following types of pronouns: (Example: First-person singular personal pronoun—*Aunt Sue gave me a telescope as a graduation present.*)
    Reflexive pronoun _____

    _____

    Second-person personal pronoun _____

    _____

    Indefinite pronoun _____

    _____

    Third-person personal pronoun (singular) _____

    _____

    Intensive pronoun _____

    _____

Critical Thinking:

3.   Why do you suppose Joe is so worried about the strange lights in the old Grizzard mansion? Give specific details or examples to support your answer.

    _____

    _____

    _____

    _____

    _____

PART ONE: WORDS

3. Verbs

The **verb** is the most important word in a sentence, because the action is in the verb. Without verbs, nothing much can happen—no dogs can *bark* at strange noises, no fish can *leap* or *swim,* no lightning can *strike* twice in the same place, no mountains can *tower* above the fruited plains. Typical verbs are *run, jump, sing, swim, shout, kick, stomp*—but the English language also contains fancier verbs such as *flabbergast, exasperate,* and *jeopardize.* Words like *sit, recline,* and *sleep* are verbs too, even though a sleeping dog is not especially active—unless he *dreams* of chasing rabbits; then he might *yelp, whine, twitch* his paws, or even *thrash* or *toss* around on the floor.

Some verbs deal not with action but with simple existence. Typical examples appear in sentences like these:

There were *three cars in the driveway.*　　　　　*My mother* is *a teacher.*
I am *in the seventh grade.*　　　　　　　　　　*You* are *my best friend.*

Verbs can also deal with appearance, with change, or with a condition of some kind:

You look *tired.*　　　　　　　　　　　*I* feel *happy.*
The ugly duckling became *a swan.*　　　*The spinach pie* tasted *terrible.*
In autumn the leaves turn *red and gold.*　*Everything* appears *normal.*

Many words can be either nouns or verbs, depending on how they are used in sentences. For example, the word *dance* is often used as a noun: "The language club will sponsor a costume *dance* on Halloween night" or "The tango is my favorite *dance.*" But *dance* is equally useful as a verb: "I love to go to a party and *dance* the night away."

Because verbs are important, they are also complicated. Every verb has many forms. For example, verbs change to show **tense** or time—that is, past, present, or future. Many English verbs form the **past tense** by adding *-d* or *-ed:* "Yesterday I *loved* you, and today I love you even more." The **future tense** is formed by adding "shall" or "will": "I *shall love* you more with every passing day." (Notice that a verb may include more than one word, as in *shall love.*) A word ending like the past-tense *-ed* is called a **suffix.** The English language has many such suffixes, including the *-s* or *-es* of plural nouns.

> **Writing Tip:** Verbs are the liveliest words in the English language.

The more strong verbs you use, the more interesting your compositions and stories will be.

Name: _____ Date: _____

ASSIGNMENT: Working with Verbs

1. Use each of the following words in two sentences, first as a noun and then as a verb:

   rain

   a. _____

   b. _____

   dream

   a. _____

   b. _____

   cook

   a. _____

   b. _____

   jump

   a. _____

   b. _____

   coach

   a. _____

   b. _____

2. Some verbs sound like what they mean. A few examples are *slap, hoot, screech, slosh,* and *buzz.* Can you think of a few more examples?

   _____

   _____

Writing Prompt: On your own paper, write a description of yourself when you are working at a favorite sport or hobby or when you are busy at some other job or activity that you perform often. When you are finished writing, circle all of the verbs.

Writing Prompt: On your own paper, write a description of a haunted house, using at least six of the following words as verbs: *swoop, swirl, flutter, flicker, hoot, howl, scream, slither, skulk, stalk, ooze, float, drift, dart, sneeze, snarl, snicker, cackle, moan.*

PART ONE: WORDS

4. More About Verbs

In addition to the simple past, present, and future tenses, English verbs also have three **perfect** tenses. "Perfect" means that the action of the verb has been completed or "perfected." The perfect tenses are easy to recognize because they always include the words *has, have,* or *had.* The **present perfect tense** describes an action that has recently been finished: "Just now I have washed the car." A **past perfect** verb indicates that the action was finished at some point in the past—maybe ten minutes ago, maybe a thousand years ago. "By three o'clock yesterday afternoon I *had mowed* the lawn." The **future perfect** tense refers to an action that will be completed at some point in the future: "By this time tomorrow I *shall have finished* my project for the science fair."

Every verb has a **present participle** (PAR-ti-sip-uhl), which is the "ing" form of the verb *(running, jumping, singing, fighting).* Each verb also has a **past participle,** which is used with the words *has, have, had, shall have,* and *will have* to form the perfect tenses.

For most verbs, the past participle looks exactly like the past tense, with an "ed" at the end *(I loved, I have loved, I had loved, I shall have loved).* A writer's life would be easy if all verbs were as simple and **regular** as the word "love." Alas, verbs are not always regular. Some verbs form the past tense and the past participle in completely illogical ways; such words are called **irregular verbs.** Here are a few examples:

> I go *to the store every day. Yesterday I* went *to the store. Just now I* have gone *to the store.*
>
> I see *a ghost. I* saw *the ghost yesterday. I* have seen *a ghost several times.*
>
> I do *homework every night. I* did *my homework last night. I* have done *today's homework already.*

Of all English verbs, the most complicated and troublesome is the verb *be,* which is completely irregular. Like a pronoun, it has first, second, and third person forms. The words *am, are, is, was, were, will be,* and *have been* look like different words, but all of them are actually forms of the same word—the verb *be.*

> **Writing Tip:** Use the correct verb tense to make your writing clear.

The present, past, past participle, and present participle are called the verb's **principal parts.** Words like *has, have,* and *had* are sometimes called "helping words," but grammarians and writers usually refer to them as **auxiliary** (awg-ZILL-yuh-ree) verbs. There are a number of auxiliary verbs in the English language, including *may, can, might, must, could, would, should, shall,* and *will.* The words *have, do,* and *be* can be used either as main verbs or as helping verbs.

The perfect tenses describe an action that has stopped, but the **progressive form** describes action that is continuing or "progressing." To form a progressive verb, use the verb *be* as an auxiliary, followed by the present participle (the "ing" form):

The basketball players are practicing *right now.*
I am studying *French this year.*
The horses were galloping *across the field.*
Joe will be playing *a trumpet solo at the band concert tonight.*

If a verb has a past tense that is different from the past participle, you should never use the past tense with an auxiliary verb. *I have did, I have saw,* and *I have went* are incorrect. On the other hand, the past participle should never be seen *without* a helping verb—for some reason, a participle needs all the help it can get. "I seen him when he done it" is terrible grammar. "I saw him when he did it" is correct.

As you can see, verbs are tricky. A chart showing all the forms of a verb is called a **conjugation** (kon-juh-GAY-shun). The chart below conjugates the verb *be* for you.

	SINGULAR	PLURAL
Present Tense		
First person	I am	We are
Second person	You are	You are
Third person	He, she, it is	They are
Past Tense		
First person	I was	We were
Second person	You were	You were
Third person	He, she, it was	They were
Future Tense		
First person	I shall be	We shall be
Second person	You will be	You will be
Third person	He, she, it will be	They will be
Present Perfect Tense		
First person	I have been	We have been
Second person	You have been	You have been
Third person	He, she, it has been	They have been
Past Perfect Tense		
First person	I had been	We had been
Second person	You had been	You had been
Third person	He, she, it had been	They had been
Future Perfect Tense		
First person	I shall have been	We shall have been
Second person	You will have been	You will have been
Third person	He, she, it will have been	They will have been

Name: _____ Date: _____

ASSIGNMENT: Thinking About Time

Critical Thinking:

1. What do you expect to be doing ten years from now? Where will you live? Where will you go every day? What will you do for fun? Explain how your future life will be different from your present life. (**Note:** For the future tense, a picky writer uses the word "shall" with *I* and *we* and "will" with everything else.)

_____

_____

_____

_____

_____

_____

_____

_____

_____

_____

2. What do you suppose it would have been like to be a cave boy or girl? What subjects would you have studied in school? (Rock-throwing and slingshot-making? Cave wall-painting?) What chores would you have done around the cave? What games would you have played? Using the past tense, describe a day in the life of a typical young cave-dweller.

_____

_____

_____

_____

_____

_____

_____

_____

_____

PART ONE: WORDS

5. Modifiers

To *modify* means to change. The superintendent of a school system might *modify* his academic calendar, for example, by adding a week-long Halloween vacation, by shortening the Christmas break from two weeks to one, or by adding classes on Saturday mornings. In the study of grammar, a **modifier** changes a word by describing it or limiting its meaning in some way. Modifiers come in two basic categories: **adjectives** and **adverbs.** Adjectives modify nouns and pronouns; adverbs modify everything else (verbs, adjectives, and other adverbs).

The usual place to find an adjective is in front of a noun:

A large, black *dog growled angrily at me.*

This loud *music is driving me crazy!*

The small *child knocked timidly on the door.*

The witness saw three *men walk stealthily into the bank.*

In the examples above, *large* and *black* modify *dog, this* and *loud* modify *music, small* modifies *child,* and *three* modifies *men.* As you can see, adjectives may indicate number, color, size, intensity, appearance, or any number of things. But not all adjectives are so descriptive. The words *a, an,* and *the* are called **articles,** and they are usually considered to be adjectives even though they don't add much to a description. The demonstrative pronouns *this, that, these,* and *those* can also be used as **demonstrative adjectives,** as in "*This* desk of mine" or "I wrote *those* songs."

> **Writing Tip:** Use the article *a* for words that begin with a consonant and *an* for words that begin with a vowel sound.

Pronouns change to show person; verbs change to show tense, and adjectives change to show **degree.** Every adjective has three degrees: **positive,** which is the basic form; **comparative,** which compares two things; and **superlative,** which compares three or more things. To form the comparative and superlative degrees of a short adjective (one syllable), use the suffixes *-er* and *-est.* For a long adjective (three or more syllables), use *more* and *most* instead. For a medium-sized adjective, you can use either method—but definitely not both. A few adjectives, such as *good* and *bad,* have irregular forms. The chart on the next page includes common positive, comparative, and superlative forms of everyday words.

Positive	Comparative	Superlative
good	better	best
bad	worse	worst
small	smaller	smallest
beautiful	more beautiful	most beautiful
friendly	friendlier more friendly	friendliest most friendly

It would be incorrect to write "more friendlier." It is also wrong to use the superlative form to compare only two people or things. Don't write "Jennifer is the *friendliest* of the two sisters." Write instead: "Jennifer is the *friendlier* (or *more friendly*) of the two sisters."

Adverbs can modify anything except nouns and pronouns, but usually they modify verbs, and they often give information about the **time** when, the **place** where, or the **manner** in which something happened. Adverbs often end with the suffix *-ly.*

A large, black dog growled angrily *at me.*

The small child knocked timidly *on the door.*

The witness saw three men walk stealthily *into the bank.*

The adverbs *not* and *never* often modify verbs: "Joe could *not* find Kristin anywhere, and he had *never* worried so much in his life." Words like *very, rather,* and *somewhat* are adverbs that modify adjectives or other adverbs:

This is a rather *big dog.*

This heron flew very *gracefully.*

The teacher speaks too *softly.*

Most adverbs form the comparative and superlative degree with *more* and *most,* as in *timidly, more timidly, most timidly.*

Note: Not every *-ly* word is an adverb. *Oily,* for example, is an adjective as in "*Oily* rags can be a fire hazard." In order to turn oily into an adverb, we would have to add another *-ly* and write a strange sentence such as "The rags lay oilily in a pile on the attic floor." Better to stick with "oily rags."

Name: _____   Date: _____

ASSIGNMENT: Working With Modifiers

Write an appropriate adverb or adjective in the blank spaces:

1. When I am at home, my _____ brother never gives me a minute's peace.

2. In a misguided effort to help mankind, Count Frankenstein created a _____ monster.

3. The dragon licked his lips _____ when he saw the _____ knight riding toward the enchanted castle on his _____ horse.

4. "Kill the umpire!" somebody shouted _____ from the bleachers, but the _____ official paid no attention.

5. Shannon is the most _____ girl in school, but her _____ sister, Kate, is a completely different sort of person.

6. That was the _____ bird I have ever seen—much _____ than the one that flew by yesterday.

7. Who is the _____ student in class?

8. The Huggins' new puppy is _____ than their old dog, but my dog Skip is the _____ of all.

9. That was my _____ time, but Jimmy was _____ than I was and won the race.

10. Susan thought that was the _____ movie we've ever seen, but I didn't think it was any _____ than *Senator Monkey*.

11. Those _____ shoes are the _____ things I've ever seen!

PART ONE: WORDS

6. Prepositions, Conjunctions, and Interjections

A **preposition** is a connecting word. Most prepositions are short words such as *in, out, under, over, above, beyond, with, without, during, until, since,* and *like.* Prepositions are always found in word groups called **prepositional phrases.** A typical prepositional phrase consists of a preposition, a noun or pronoun, and perhaps an adjective or two: *in the house, out the door, above the clouds, beyond the fence, with my friends, without me, during lunch, until noon, since last week.* Notice that many of these phrases deal with space or time. The noun or pronoun at the end of the phrase is called the **object of the preposition.**

Prepositional phrases usually serve as adjectives or adverbs—that is, they modify or describe nouns and verbs.

The man in the red truck *is my biology teacher. (Adjective modifying* man.*)*

I enjoy a movie with a happy ending. *(Adjective modifying* movie.*)*

The cat crawled under the house. *(Adverb modifying* crawled.*)*

The plane flew above the clouds. *(Adverb modifying* flew.*)*

Occasionally a prepositional phrase is used as a noun:

During lunch *is when I visit my friends.*

Beyond the fence *is out of bounds.*

Under the piano *is where my dog likes to sleep.*

> **Writing Tip:** Do not end sentences with prepositions.

Most prepositions are short words, but a few prepositions consist of two or three words. These are called **group prepositions:**

Peter went into the forest in spite of *his grandfather's warning.*

The school bus was waiting in front of *the gym.*

> **Writing Tip:** Do not begin or end sentences with conjunctions.

Another kind of connecting word is the **conjunction.** Typical conjunctions are *and, but, or, nor, for, yet,* and *so.*

Alice and *Jim are working together on their science project this weekend.*

I pounded on the door, but *it was locked.*

I can come to your apartment, or *we can meet at the theatre.*

Everyone is familiar with the **interjection,** a word or phrase that expresses emotion:

Ouch! *I cut my finger.*

Whoopee! *The Cubs win the division!*

Arrgh! *The dog ate my computer discs!*

Well, *I think I'll go home now.*

Oh, *let's forget about homework and go to a movie tonight.*

Interjections are used to add excitement, surprise, or fear to your writing to help the reader connect with the characters more. A sentence like "The dog ate my homework," is a grammatically correct sentence, but it doesn't tell us, the readers, how the writer feels about it. We can't tell if the dog really ate the homework, or if it's just an excuse because the writer didn't do the homework. By adding the "Arrgh!" we know that the writer is upset, which leads us to conclude that the dog really did eat the homework.

> **Writing Tip:** Use interjections sparingly. Overusing interjections makes the reader feel like the writer is shouting at them.

Punctuation note: A comma is a mark of punctuation that is used to separate or set off words and phrases. Notice that a mild interjection is followed by a comma and that a stronger interjection takes an exclamation point. "Oh! I forgot!" has a stronger emotional meaning than, "Oh, I forgot."

Nouns, pronouns, verbs, adjectives, adverbs, prepositions, and interjections are called the **parts of speech.** These are the building blocks with which a writer constructs sentences, paragraphs, articles, stories, and books.

Name: _____ Date: _____

ASSIGNMENT: Parts of Speech

In the blank space at the left, identify each underlined word by its part of speech.

Example: _verb_   *The lion chased the unicorn through the dark forest.*

1. _____   Robin Hood and his merry men <u>robbed</u> the rich and gave to the poor.

2. _____   We can work for hours to prepare an elegant meal, <u>or</u> we can order a pizza and eat on paper plates.

3. _____   <u>Yipes</u>! I have three tests tomorrow, and I haven't opened a book since Halloween.

4. _____   This is the <u>longest</u> speech I have ever heard.

5. _____   <u>Benjamin Franklin</u> was a scientist, an inventor, a writer, and a states-man.

6. _____   I was sick with worry when my dog jumped <u>over</u> the fence and ran into the woods.

7. _____   This book is difficult to read because the sentences are <u>very</u> long.

8. _____   Dorothy sank <u>sleepily</u> down upon the field of deadly poppies and fell into a heavy slumber.

9. _____   On Friday night Brian <u>will play</u> a trumpet solo at the annual Homecoming concert.

10. _____   Lady was the <u>most beautiful</u> dog in the show, but she performed poorly in the obedience trials.

11. _____   Growing <u>sunflowers</u> is easy—you should try it.

12. _____   Larry <u>and</u> Penny went to the park to shoot hoops.

13. _____   I was impressed by <u>the</u> artist's attention to detail.

14. _____   Brian <u>scored</u> the winning goal in the game this weekend.

15. _____   The ancient car lurched <u>haltingly</u> to the side of the road.

PART TWO: SENTENCES

7. Subjects, Verbs, and Compounds

A writer builds sentences out of words. In order to qualify as a **sentence,** a group of words must meet two basic requirements:

1. It must make sense or express a complete idea.

2. It must contain both a subject and a verb.

Because it is impossible to express a sensible idea about nothing, every sentence must have a **subject,** which is always some kind of noun or pronoun. The **verb** makes a statement about the subject. Just as a carpenter builds a house on a frame, a writer builds a sentence on a **subject-verb combination.** The simplest kind of sentence would consist of nothing except a subject and a verb:

Dogs barked.

This group of words does not give us much information, but it does at least make sense, and it definitely contains a subject (dogs) and a verb (barked). Therefore, it qualifies as a sentence. If we wish to include more information, we can add adjectives, adverbs, and prepositional phrases:

> **Writing Tip:** Every sentence you write must make sense.

The brave guard dogs barked loudly and ferociously at the evil burglars.

But no matter how many modifiers we add, the basic frame of the sentence remains the same: the subject (dogs) and the verb (barked). Even if you remove all the modifiers, the sentence still makes sense.

Verbs rarely stand alone; they are usually accompanied by modifiers. Taken together, the verb and all of its modifiers form a unit that is sometimes called the **predicate** or the **complete predicate.** Consider our sentence again:

> **Writing Tip:** Always make sure every sentence you write has a subject and a verb.

The brave guard dogs barked loudly and ferociously at the evil burglars.

The predicate is "barked loudly and ferociously at the evil burglars."

Sometimes a sentence may have two subjects, as in *"Martha and I* are taking clarinet lessons."* In fact, any element of a sentence may be double or **compound:**

The guard dogs barked and growled. (compound verb)

The guard dogs barked loudly and growled ferociously. (complete predicate is compound)

The small but ferocious dogs barked at the burglars. (compound adjective)

The dogs barked loudly and ferociously. (compound adverb)

The dogs chased the burglars out of the house and down the street. (compound prepositional phrase)

We must sink or swim. (compound verb)

Even the sentence itself may be compound.

The dogs barked ferociously, but the burglars paid no attention.

A group of three or more nouns, verbs, or modifiers is called a **series:**

Dogs, cats, rabbits, and horses make good pets. (series of nouns)

The angry dogs barked, growled, and whined. (series of verbs)

The American flag is red, white, and blue. (series of adjectives)

Notice that where you find a compound or a series, you will usually find a joining word or **conjunction** nearby. Often that conjunction is the word *and, but,* or *or.*

Punctuation note: Remember that a **comma** is used to separate or enclose words or phrases. In the examples above, notice that a careful writer will (a) use a comma before the conjunction in a compound sentence and (b) use commas to separate the items in a series.

> **WritingTip:** Only use one conjunction in a series or list. That conjunction comes between the last two items in the series.

Name: _____   Date: _____

ASSIGNMENT: Subjects, Verbs, and Compounds

Write sentences containing the following items. Be sure to use commas correctly.

Example: Series of three proper nouns:

 <u>Joe, Kristin, and Coach Wilson</u> stayed after school.

1. A compound subject and one verb:

     _____

2. A series of three adjectives:

     _____

3. A compound prepositional phrase:

     _____

4. One subject and a series of three verbs:

     _____

5. A compound adverb:

     _____

6. A compound sentence:

     _____

     _____

7. A sentence with three subjects:

     _____

8. A compound sentence containing a compound prepositional phrase:

     _____

     _____

9. A compound sentence containing a list:

     _____

     _____

10. A sentence with two subjects and two verbs:

     _____

PART TWO: SENTENCES

8. Direct Objects

To create interesting sentences, a writer needs more than subjects, verbs, and modifiers. An especially useful type of word is the **direct object,** which is always some kind of noun or pronoun. In a normal English sentence, the direct object follows the verb and answers the question *Whom?* or *What?* Usually the subject of the sentence does something to the direct object:

Andy kicked the football.
  (What did Andy kick? The football.)
I saw a werewolf.
  (What did I see? A werewolf.)
Mary loves everyone.
  (Whom does Mary love? Everyone.)
The car was dirty, so I washed it.
  (What did I wash? It—that is, the car.)

Sometimes the subject is a person who makes or creates the direct object:

Mother baked cookies.
Beethoven wrote music.
The pioneer built a cabin *in the woods.*
The pirate drew a map *of Treasure Island.*

Note: The direct object is part of the **complete predicate.** Like any noun, a direct object can have modifiers: *I saw an ugly werewolf with sharp fangs.*

Once in a while, the subject gives or presents the direct object to someone. In such a case, the sentence will have an **indirect object** as well as a direct object:

Mother gave me *a bicycle for my birthday.*
The teacher told her students *a story.*

If a verb has a direct object, grammarians say that the verb is **transitive,** because its action is *transferred* from the subject to the direct object. A verb with no direct object (as in the sentence *Dogs barked)* is called **intransitive.**

When the subject, transitive verb, and direct object are in their normal positions, a grammarian would say that the verb is in **active voice.** However, a transitive verb has the special ability to turn itself

> **Writing Tip:** Remember, a direct object is always a noun or pronoun.

wrong-side out. For example, *"Andy kicked the football"* can become *"The football was kicked by Andy." "Beethoven wrote music"* can become *"Music was written by Beethoven."* In both of these examples, the direct objects *(football* and *music)* turn into subjects.

When this happens, we say that the verb is in **passive voice.** A writer forms the passive voice by using *be* as an auxiliary with the past participle of the main verb.

ACTIVE VOICE: *Mother baked cookies.*
PASSIVE VOICE: *Cookies were baked by Mother.*

ACTIVE VOICE: *I saw a werewolf.*
PASSIVE VOICE: *A werewolf was seen by me.*

As you can see from the examples above, passive verbs are wordy. Furthermore, a sentence with a passive verb is tame and dull, because the subject does nothing on its own. It just sits there. Better to have your subjects get up and do things: kick footballs, bake cookies, write music, draw maps.

> **Writing Tip:** Use as many active verbs as possible.

There are three instances where the passive voice has a place in your writing. You can use passive voice when you do not know who or what the subject is.

> *The bike was stolen on Thursday.* (*by someone* is understood)

You can also use the passive voice when everyone understands who or what the subject is.

> *The thief was arrested on Friday.* (*by the police* is understood, because the police are the only people who arrest thieves)

Finally, you can use the passive voice when you do not want to emphasize the subject in the sentence.

> *The thief was convicted by a jury of his peers.* (This sentence could read *A jury of his peers convicted the thief,* but the writer wants to emphasize *the thief,* not *the jury*.)

Some styles of scientific writing require passive voice, so it is important to know what it is and how to use it. However, if every sentence in your paper has a *was* and a *by* in it, you are overusing the passive voice. Remember, using the active voice makes your writing stronger and easier to read.

Name: _____   Date: _____

ASSIGNMENT: Direct Objects

Fill in each blank with a good direct object:

1. Of all my subjects in school, I especially like _____.

2. Some people like dogs and cats, but I want _____ for a pet.

3. On her way home, Jennifer bought some _____ at the grocery store.

4. The escaped convict drove his stolen car off the road and struck _____.

5. When I get to high school, I want to play _____ in the school orchestra.

Use each of the following words as direct objects in a sentence. If you like, your direct objects can have modifiers.

Example: <u>contest</u>: My brother won the sixth-grade spelling contest last week.

1. elephant _____

2. saxophone _____

3. truck _____

4. turkey _____

5. robot _____

Writing Prompt:
Writers love transitive verbs because they are full of action, and action makes for exciting articles and stories. Using as many transitive verbs as possible, write a description of one of the following: an exciting football, basketball, or hockey game; a crazy party; a bank robbery; a Thanksgiving feast; a noisy parade. When you are finished, circle every direct object.

_____

_____

_____

_____

_____

_____

PART TWO: SENTENCES

9. Subjective Complements

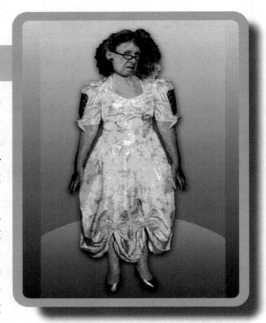

Sometimes a sentence has a **subjective complement** instead of a direct object. The subjective complement gets its name because it **completes** the subject. (Notice that in the study of grammar, the word *complement* is spelled differently from *compliment,* a word that means "an expression of praise.")

A subjective complement always follows the verb. For this reason, it is occasionally mistaken for a direct object. But unlike a direct object, a subjective complement can sometimes be an adjective instead of a noun or pronoun. Another important difference is that a subject and a direct object are almost always two different people or things, but the subjective complement refers back to the subject of the sentence. If the complement is a noun, it renames the subject; if the complement is an adjective, it modifies the subject.

My brother is an idiot. (My brother and the idiot are the same person.)

Griselda's dress looks hideous. (The word *hideous* describes the dress.)

The choir sounds flat. (Flat describes the singing of the choir.)

Dracula became a vampire. (Dracula and the vampire are the same creature.)

The subject and its complement are connected by a special verb called a **linking verb.** Linking verbs come in three types:

1. Forms of the verb *be* (such as *were, am, will be, have been,* as in *"My brother is an idiot.")*

2. Verbs that refer to the senses—*look, sound, smell, feel,* and *taste,* as in *"The choir sounds flat"* and *"Griselda's dress looks hideous."*

3. Other verbs such as *seem, become, appear, turn,* and *grow,* as in *"Dracula became a vampire."*

If you can remember the three basic types of verbs—**transitive, intransitive,** and **linking**—you can understand the framework of almost any English sentence. These are the three basic **sentence patterns** of the English language:

> **Writing Tip:** Remember, a subjective complement always follows the verb.

1. **Subject—Intransitive Verb**
2. **Subject—Transitive Verb—Direct Object**
3. **Subject—Linking Verb—Subjective Complement**

Every English sentence, no matter how complicated, is built upon one of these patterns. Keep in mind, however, that some verbs can be either transitive, intransitive, or linking, depending on how they are used in sentences.

Transitive Verb: *The Phantom's hand turned the pages of the strange manuscript.*
  (*pages* is the direct object)

Intransitive Verb: *The wagon wheels turned slowly as the pioneers traveled west.*
  (no direct object)

Linking Verb: *When autumn came, the leaves turned gold.*
  (*gold* is the complement; it describes *leaves*)

When a subjective complement is a noun, grammarians sometimes call it a **predicate nominative** or **predicate noun.** (Grammarians love big words.) An adjective complement may be called a **predicate adjective.** Regardless of the name, a subjective complement is always a part of the **complete predicate,** just as a direct object is.

A NOTE ON GRAMMAR: It is fortunate that the English language has only a few personal pronouns, because they are almost as tricky as verbs. Unlike other English words, some of the personal pronouns change form to show **case**—that is, to show whether they are subjects or objects. Here is a brief guide to the use of pronoun case forms:

NOMINATIVE CASE: I, he, she, we, they, who, whoever. Use these words as **subjects** or **subjective complements only.**

OBJECTIVE CASE: me, him, her, us, them, whom, whomever. Use these words as **direct objects, indirect objects,** or **objects of prepositions.**

Name: _____ Date: _____

ASSIGNMENT: Types of Verbs

Write sentences using the following verbs. Use whatever tense you like. If you include pronouns, be careful to use the correct case.

1. *hit* as a transitive verb

_____

2. *seem* as a linking verb

_____

3. *dance* as an intransitive verb

_____

4. *see* as a transitive verb

_____

5. *become* as a linking verb

_____

6. *bounce* as an intransitive verb

_____

7. *run* as an intransitive verb

_____

8. *taste* as a linking verb

_____

9. *grow* as a linking verb

_____

10. *am* as a linking verb

_____

11. *strike* as an intransitive verb

_____

PART TWO: SENTENCES

10. Verbals

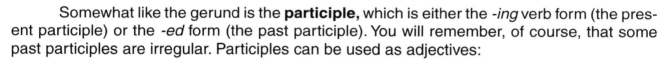

Some verb forms can be used as other parts of speech—as nouns, adjectives, and adverbs instead of as verbs. Such words are called **verbals.** They are made from verbs, but they are not true verbs because they lack subjects.

Such a verbal is the **gerund** (JEH-rund), which is easy to recognize because it always includes the suffix *-ing*. A gerund is used as a noun, and it can do anything a noun can do:

Traveling *is fun.* (gerund as subject)
I hate studying. (gerund as direct object)
My favorite sport is swimming.
    (gerund as subjective complement)
Some people earn money by writing. (gerund as object of preposition)

Somewhat like the gerund is the **participle,** which is either the *-ing* verb form (the present participle) or the *-ed* form (the past participle). You will remember, of course, that some past participles are irregular. Participles can be used as adjectives:

The dancing *bear was the hit of the circus.*
The defeated *boxer was a poor loser.*
A broken *heart is painful.* (*Broken* is the past participle of *break*.)

As you can see, the *-ing* verb form can be either a gerund or a participle, depending on whether it is used as a noun (a gerund) or an adjective (a participle).

I enjoy dancing. (gerund as direct object)
The dancing *bear is performing now.* (participle)

The third verbal is the **infinitive.** An infinitive is a combination of a verb with the word *to,* the so-called "sign of the infinitive": *to run, to be, to love, to have loved, to be loved.* Infinitives can be used as nouns, adjectives, or adverbs:

> **Writing Tip:** Remember, gerunds, participles, and infinitives are verbals that can be nouns, adjectives, or adverbs, but not verbs.

I hate to study. (infinitive as noun—direct object)
To fail *is painful.* (infinitive as noun—subject)
My goal is to succeed. (infinitive as noun—subjective complement)
I have found a good book to read. (infinitive as adjective—modifies *book*)
The Springfield Panthers play to win. (infinitive as adverb—modifies *play*)
Good grades are hard to get. (infinitive as adverb—modifies *hard*)

Obviously, verbs have many uses. If a writer wants to excel, he or she must learn to make good use of verbs and all of their forms.

Name: _____ Date: _____

ASSIGNMENT: Verbals

In each sentence, identify the underlined verbal as a gerund, participle, *or* infinitive:

1. _____ The policemen chased a <u>speeding</u> car through the center of town at high speeds.

2. _____ *The Werewolf's Grandmother* is the best movie <u>to see</u> this summer.

3. _____ <u>Jogging</u> always makes me hungry and thirsty.

4. _____ This party is boring, and I want <u>to leave</u> right now.

5. _____ The <u>sobbing</u> child trembled and threw her arms around her mother.

6. _____ <u>Burned</u> toast makes a terrible breakfast.

7. _____ Nothing is quite as beautiful as a <u>galloping</u> horse.

8. _____ <u>Eating</u> has always been Dolly's only hobby.

9. _____ My fondest wish is <u>to be appreciated</u> for what I am.

10. _____ After the earthquake, the streets were covered with <u>shattered</u> glass and broken pieces of wood.

11. _____ Peter Pan had the remarkable ability <u>to fly</u>.

12. _____ The rats had chewed everything and left a <u>disgusting</u> mess.

13. _____ Franklin said that fish and guests begin <u>to smell</u> after three days.

14. _____ Everyone says that it is foolish <u>to cry</u> over spilled milk.

15. _____ But I enjoy <u>crying</u>, and spilled milk is as good an excuse as any.

16. _____ I want <u>to see</u> what you are talking about before you buy any new car.

17. _____ The sound of <u>laughing</u> children filled the air around the puppet show.

18. _____ The mayor's reelection campaign slogan is "<u>Working</u> for Quincy."

19. _____ All I want for my birthday is <u>to get</u> a new skateboard.

20. _____ <u>Catching</u> a cold is something I try to avoid doing.

PART TWO: SENTENCES

11. Phrases

Just as people will sometimes join together to form a team or a club, words often cluster together and form a unit—a noun, a verb, an adjective, or an adverb. One familiar type of word cluster is the **phrase.** A phrase is different from a complete sentence because (1) a phrase does not contain a subject-verb combination, and (2) a phrase does not make sense by itself. Instead, it always functions as part of a larger sentence.

You are already familiar with the **prepositional phrase,** which consists of a preposition, an object, and any modifiers of the object. A prepositional phrase serves as either an adjective, an adverb, or (on rare occasions) a noun.

The cat hid *under the bed.* (adverb)

The woman *in the red suit* is my mother. (adjective)

Over the rainbow is where I'd like to be. (noun)

Remember, a typical prepositional phrase consists of a preposition, a noun or pronoun, and perhaps an adjective or two. The noun or pronoun at the end of the phrase is called the **object of the preposition.**

There are many other kinds of phrases. The most common kind of phrase is when a verb and its auxiliaries join together to form a **verb phrase:**

> **Writing Tip:** Remember, don't end a sentence with a preposition. However, you can end a sentence with a prepositional phrase.

The soccer team *has been practicing* since April.

Joe *has loved* the game of soccer all his life.

I *have seen* every one of his games.

What *have* you *been doing* since I saw you last?

I *have been spending* a lot of time at the beach.

Grammar note: Adverbs such as *not, never, sometimes, always,* and *seldom* often appear between a verb and its auxiliaries: has *not* loved, has *never* loved, has *always* loved, has *seldom* loved. Such adverbs are not part of the verb phrase; they are strictly modifiers.

I *have* never *seen* that new game show, *Bet the Farm.*

You will remember the **gerund**, an *-ing* verb form that serves as a noun. Because the gerund is a form of a verb, it can have a direct object, a subjective complement, or adverbs of its own. When a gerund is accompanied by related words, it becomes a **gerund phrase:**

I hate studying history. (a gerund and a direct object)

Holly enjoys looking beautiful. (a gerund and a subjective complement)

Marvin's favorite pastime is happily playing baseball with his friends. (a gerund, an object, and modifiers. Notice that a prepositional phrase, *with his friends,* is included within the gerund phrase.)

What I hate worst is waiting for hours in a doctor's reception room filled with forty sneezing children and sixty billion germs. (a long gerund phrase)

Like gerunds, participles and infinitives can have objects, complements, or modifiers:

The woman wearing the red suit *is my mother.* (participle phrase)

Looking like a queen, *Holly walked onto the stage.* (participle phrase)

I hate to study history. (infinitive phrase as direct object)

To win a beauty pageant *is Holly's dream.* (infinitive phrase as subject)

A bouquet of roses is a good present to give on Mother's Day.
    (infinitive phrase as an adjective modifying *present.*)

Carrie works hard to impress her teachers. (infinitive phrase modifying *works*)

Gerund phrases, participle phrases, and infinitive phrases are also known as **verbal phrases.**

Name: _____ Date: _____

ASSIGNMENT: Types of Phrases

Identify each underlined element as a *prepositional phrase, verb phrase, gerund phrase, participle phrase,* or *infinitive phrase.* You may use abbreviations for each term on the blanks if needed.

1. _____ Swimming every day is a good way <u>to get exercise</u>.

2. _____ Julia won the talent contest by <u>playing a trumpet solo</u>.

3. _____ Here is the information <u>to learn for the test</u>.

4. _____ The frightened horse leaped <u>over the high pasture fence</u>.

5. _____ The bus <u>should be arriving</u> at any minute.

6. _____ I don't enjoy <u>waiting in the rain for the bus</u>.

7. _____ Now is the time <u>to clean the basement</u>.

8. _____ <u>After the hockey game</u>, everyone went to the ice cream shop.

9. _____ The man <u>playing the piano</u> is also a good singer.

10. _____ My goal in life is <u>to become a doctor</u>.

11. _____ I'm leaving now, and don't try <u>to stop me</u>.

12. _____ <u>To dance well</u> takes time and practice.

13. _____ <u>Sleeping through class</u> is a good way to make the teacher angry.

14. _____ Delbert <u>must have been sleeping</u> through Coach Wilson's class.

15. _____ Now Delbert is hiding <u>in the locker room</u> from Coach Wilson.

16. _____ The locker room is probably not the best place <u>to hide safely</u>.

17. _____ Lockers <u>in locker rooms</u> aren't usually big enough to hide in.

18. _____ Of course, they also tend <u>to smell like last year's gym socks</u>.

19. _____ Where else could Delbert hide <u>in a locker room</u>, though?

20. _____ <u>In no time</u>, Coach Wilson found Delbert; he was hiding behind some equipment.

PART TWO: SENTENCES

12. Types of Sentences: Declarative, Interrogative, Imperative, and Exclamatory

Sentences come in different types. Probably the most common type of sentence is the **declarative** sentence, which makes a statement. When you write reports for class, most of your sentences will be declarative:

The American flag is red, white, and blue.

George Washington was the first president of the United States.

I have a bad cold today.

Classes begin at eight o'clock in the morning.

Peter Pan flew out the window.

An **imperative** sentence is a command or a request. The subject of an imperative sentence is frequently understood to be "you;" therefore, it is unnecessary to include "you" in the sentence.

Shut the door. (the subject *you* is understood)

Sally, please pass the steak sauce. (*Sally* is the subject)

Drive carefully. (the subject *you* is understood)

Bob, get out of my house this minute! (*Bob* is the subject)

The word *imperative* is closely related to the words *imperial* and *emperor*—an emperor would probably give a lot of commands during a typical day. But most imperative sentences are polite rather than bossy. Recipes, instruction manuals, useful advice, and self-help books and articles are often expressed in imperative sentences.

> **Writing Tip:** If you are writing a how-to essay, make sure all your imperative sentences are polite.

To become a good pianist, set aside time to practice every day. Begin by playing scales and keyboard exercises for at least ten minutes. Remember to keep your fingers curved and to sit erect at the keyboard. Don't slouch or slump. After you have completed your exercises, try playing a simple piece of music.

An **interrogative** (in-ter-ROG-a-tive) sentence asks a question:

Are you awake?

When does the movie start?

Who discovered the Mississippi River?

What is a subjective complement?

An **exclamatory** sentence expresses strong emotion. Note that a true exclamation has a different word order from that of a simple declarative sentence:

What a terrible movie this is!

How beautiful you look tonight!

That's awful!

What a pity!

Punctuation note: A declarative sentence always ends with a period, and so does an imperative sentence—unless the command is especially forceful, as in "Run for your life!" An interrogative sentence ends with a question mark, and an exclamatory sentence ends with an exclamation point.

An exclamation point can turn an ordinary declarative sentence into an exclamation (as in "The Cubs won the division!"), but beware! Exclamation points scattered everywhere will give your writing an hysterical tone. For the most part, stick to declarative sentences, and save the exclamation points for occasions of genuinely strong feeling.

Name: _____   Date: _____

ASSIGNMENT: Types of Sentences

Identify each of the following sentences as *declarative, imperative, interrogative,* or *exclamatory:*

1. _____ Huckleberry Finn and his friend Jim sailed down the Mississippi River on a raft.

2. _____ Please face the microphone and speak slowly so that everyone can understand you.

3. _____ Do you really think it's a good idea for the organist to play "The Stars and Stripes Forever" at Aunt Gussy's funeral?

4. _____ I enjoy eating almost any foods except Brussels sprouts, turnip greens, and octopus tentacles.

5. _____ What a long, complicated test that was!

6. _____ Heat two tablespoons of oil in a skillet, and add the onions, peppers, and spices.

7. _____ I want to go home right now.

8. _____ Have you ever read *Treasure Island* by Robert Louis Stevenson?

9. _____ E. B. White was the author of *Charlotte's Web* and several other books.

10. _____ How I would love to have a banana split right at this very minute!

11. _____ I had a banana split for lunch.

12. _____ What are you doing?

13. _____ Who is that masked man?

14. _____ What do you think you are doing, coming home so late after curfew?

15. _____ Open the program, and then click on the drop-down menu and select the photo you want to edit.

Writing Prompt: *On your own paper, write instructions on how to do something—take a good photograph, bake a cake, care for a pet, get in practice for football, or whatever you know how to do. Use imperative sentences.*

PART THREE: CLAUSES

13. Independent Clauses

Like a phrase, a **clause** is a group of related words. However, unlike a phrase, a clause always contains a subject-verb combination—at least one subject and at least one verb. If a clause makes enough sense to stand alone as a complete sentence, it is called an **independent clause.**

Kevin lit the lantern.

Laurie unfolded the map.

A dog howled in the distance.

A **simple sentence** consists of only one independent clause. When two or more independent clauses are joined by a **coordinating conjunction,** the result is a **compound sentence.** There are seven coordinating conjunctions in the English language: *and, but, or, nor, for, yet,* and *so.*

Kevin lit the lantern, and *Laurie unfolded the map.*

Laurie was nervous, but *she held the map steady.*

A dog howled in the distance, or *maybe it was a wolf.*

Kevin and Laurie had never been inside the shack before, nor *had they ever seen such a peculiar map.*

Kevin and Laurie were bewildered, for *the map seemed to be written in a strange language.*

Kevin was tired, yet *he continued working.*

The sky was growing dark, so *Laurie went home.*

> **Writing Tip:** In a compound sentence, a comma comes before the conjunction.

Independent clauses can come in series as well as in compounds:

Kevin lit the lantern, Laurie unfolded the map, and both of them tried to read the strange handwriting.

Note: The word *plus* should not be used as a substitute for the word *and.*

Wrong: *Laurie had to finish her homework for three classes,* plus *she had to bake cookies for her Girl Scout picnic.*

Correct: *Laurie had to finish her homework for three classes,* and *she had to bake cookies for her Girl Scout picnic.*

Independent clauses can also be joined by word pairs called **correlative conjunctions:** *not only. . . but also, either. . . or,* and *neither. . . nor.*

Not only *did Laurie have to finish her homework for three classes,* but *she* also *had to bake cookies for her Girl Scout picnic.*

Either *we can go to a movie,* or *we can stay home and watch television.*

Note: Correlative conjunctions can join other compounds besides sentences:

Neither *Kevin* nor *Laurie could read the map.*

Both *the map* and *the ring looked old.*

Occasionally a simple sentence begins with a coordinating conjunction:

Kevin had been working all day, and he was tired. Yet *he continued to search for the map.*

But don't get in the habit of starting every sentence with a conjunction, or your writing will start to sound jumpy.

When you join two independent clauses to form a compound sentence, those clauses should have some kind of logical relationship. *Kevin lit the lantern, and Laurie unfolded the map* is fine: Kevin and Laurie will need light in order to read the map. But consider this sentence: *Laurie unfolded the map, and a spider crawled across the ceiling.* That spider might add to the scariness of the situation, but the two clauses do not belong together in the same sentence, because there is no real connection between the map and the spider.

> **Writing Tip:** Good writing uses a mix of simple and compound sentences to keep the reader interested.

Name: _____   Date: _____

ASSIGNMENT: Working With Compounds

The following passage is dull and difficult to understand because it contains nothing except short, simple sentences. Rewrite the passage using compound subjects, verbs, and sentences wherever you can.

Kevin opened the door of the shack. He went inside. Laurie followed him. They looked around. The shack was dark. It was also cold. Everything was covered with dust. The air smelled musty. Kevin tried not to sneeze. A spider crawled across the ceiling. Laurie shivered. She wondered whether the spider was poisonous. In the distance a dog began to howl. The wind rattled the old window panes.

There was no furniture except a desk. Kevin brushed some of the dust off of the desk. He opened the top drawer. He saw a yellowed piece of paper inside. Laurie noticed a ring lying beside the paper. The ring looked tarnished. The jewels in the ring still sparkled faintly.

The sun was about to set. Kevin decided to light the lantern. Laurie unfolded the paper. She stared in surprise. It looked like a map of Summer Cove. She could not read the words on the map. Kevin could not read the words either. The map seemed to be written in a foreign language.

_____

_____

_____

_____

_____

_____

_____

_____

_____

_____

_____

_____

_____

PART THREE: CLAUSES

14. Adverb Clauses

Suppose your teacher were to walk into class one day and make the following announcement:

Because some of you did so badly on the last test. Who has decided to hold three extra study sessions. Whoever scored below fifty. When you should plan to attend at least one session. If you have many questions. Who will give a second test after Thanksgiving. Which will help you improve your grades.

It is possible to make a little sense out of this speech—apparently the teacher plans to give some extra attention to the students who did poorly on the last test—but still, the teacher sounds as if he has lost his mind. The reason that his announcement seems so garbled is that he is speaking in **dependent clauses** instead of sentences. A dependent clause contains a subject and a verb, but it does not make sense by itself.

Like a phrase, a dependent clause (also called a **subordinate clause**) serves within a larger sentence as a single part of speech—either an adverb, an adjective, or a noun. As its name implies, an **adverb clause** usually modifies a verb. Most of the time, an adverb clause is easy to recognize because it contains at least one subject, at least one verb, and a **subordinating conjunction** to introduce the clause or join it to the main part of the sentence. Typical subordinating conjunctions are *when, before, after, until, where, so that, wherever, because, as, unless, although, if, as if,* and *even if.*

> **Writing Tip:** A dependent clause must be joined to a complete sentence.

An adverb clause can describe a verb in many ways. For example, the clause can indicate the *time* of the action, the *place* of the action, the *cause* of the action, or the *manner* in which the action took place.

Kevin went home when the sun set. (time)

The map had been hidden where only a clever person could find it. (place)

Laurie shivered because she was cold. (cause)

The dog howled as if he was lonely. (manner)

Notice that when the adverb clause comes at the end of a sentence, no punctuation is required to join it to the sentence.

However, when a long adverb clause (eight words or more) appears at the beginning of a sentence, it should be set off by a comma:

Because the map was written in a foreign language, *Laurie and Kevin decided to show it to their French teacher.*

Unless you practice for at least an hour every day, *you will never become a skilled pianist.*

This same advice applies to long participle phrases that appear at the beginning of a sentence:

Streaking through the skies as fast as he could go, *Peter Pan sped to rescue Wendy.*

Running as if he had seen a bloodthirsty monster, *Kevin fled through the dark woods.* (Notice that an adverb clause is included within the participle phrase.)

If you like, you can also set off short introductory modifiers with a comma:

When the sun set, *Kevin went home.*
Feeling cold, *Laurie shivered.*

A good general rule of thumb to remember is that when a dependent clause of any kind comes at the beginning of a sentence, you need a comma to join it to the rest of the sentence.

Name: _____   Date: _____

ASSIGNMENT: Adverb Clauses

Fill in each blank space with an appropriate adverb clause. The subordinating conjunction is already provided. Be sure to include any necessary punctuation.

Example: When *the full moon rises over the dark woods,* the werewolves begin to howl.

1. The bank robbers will be captured and sent to jail unless _____.

2. Marvin practiced playing the piccolo until _____.

3. Biff fumbled the football because _____.

4. If _____ I will go to hear the Singing Zombies perform at the Lakeside Auditorium.

5. Whenever _____ Mr. Mullins loses his temper.

6. Although _____ Mindy won first prize at the violin festival.

7. Unless _____ I will never get this work done.

8. Holly walked onto the stage and danced as if _____.

9. When _____ I will move to Hawaii.

10. I quit my job at the Greasy Pizza Factory because _____.

11. I will go to the concert after _____.

12. Hal's Hamburger Heaven is a place where _____.

13. If _____ my friends and I will be excited.

14. I will eat ice cream tonight unless _____.

15. The amusement park is a good place to visit even if _____

_____.

16. Whenever _____ I'm so happy that I hope the day will never end.

17. They treated Kali as if _____.

18. Before _____, Sara had to go home.

19. My friends and I have fun wherever _____.

20. Although _____, I want to do my very best.

PART THREE: CLAUSES

14. Adjective Clauses

An **adjective clause** modifies or defines a noun or pronoun. An adjective clause is usually introduced by a **relative word:** *who, whom, whose, that, which, when,* or *where.* These are called *relative* words because they connect or "relate" the clause to the rest of the sentence.

> *Laurie and Kevin found a map* that was written in a strange language.
>
> *The old shack was the place* where they found the map.
>
> *Laurie,* who was a good language student, *decided to show the map to her teacher.*
>
> *The teacher was a man* whom Laurie and Kevin had known all their lives.

Notice that a relative word also functions as a part of speech *within* its adjective clause. In the second example above, the word *where* modifies *found,* and in the third example, *who* is the subject of the verb *was.*

Adjective clauses come in two types: restrictive and non-restrictive. A **restrictive clause** is necessary in order for the sentence to make sense, or is at least necessary to identify the noun. (That is, it "restricts" the noun or pronoun.)

> *Anyone* who finds the lost dog *should call the humane society.* (Not just "anyone" should call—only a person who has found the dog.)
>
> *All students* who are participating in the choir concert *will be excused from class on Friday.* (Not "all students"—only the members of the choir.)
>
> *A dog* that bites people *makes a poor pet.* (Not "any dog"—just one that bites.)
>
> *I admire a man* who knows when to keep his mouth shut. (Not just any man—only a silent type.)

A **non-restrictive clause** adds information or description, but such a clause is not necessary in order to identify the noun.

> *Laurie,* who was a good language student, *decided to show the map to her teacher.* (No restrictive clause is needed because Laurie is identified by name.)
>
> *My birthplace,* which is a small town in Texas, *recently celebrated its centennial.* (A person can only have one birthplace.)

> **Writing Tip:** Remember, an adjective clause is usually introduced by a relative word: *who, whom, whose, that, which, when,* or *where.*

My best friend, who lives on a farm, *is coming to visit me in Chicago next week.* (A person can have a thousand friends but only one "best" friend.)

I admire Herbert Throckmorton, who knows when to keep his mouth shut. (Mr. Throckmorton is identified by name.)

Note: Participle phrases can be non-restrictive too:

Herbert Throckmorton, keeping his mouth shut, *listened to everything that was said at the meeting.*

Punctuation note: As you can see from the examples above, a non-restrictive clause is set off by commas, but a restrictive clause is not. Notice also that when a non-restrictive clause appears in the middle of a sentence, two commas are needed, not just one.

Wrong: *Laurie who was a good language student, decided to show the map to her teacher.*

Also wrong: *Laurie, who was a good language student decided to show the map to her teacher.*

A note about relative words: The words *who* and *whom* refer to people; the words *that* and *which* usually refer to animals and objects. The word *that* should be used in restrictive clauses. The word *which* should be saved for non-restrictive clauses.

> **Writing Tip:** If you do not need commas to set off your clause, it is a restrictive clause and you use *that.* If you need commas to set off your clause, it is a non-restrictive clause and you use *which*.

The movie that *was on TV last night is my favorite.* (restrictive clause)

<u>*Batman*</u>, which *was on TV last night, is my favorite movie.* (non-restrictive clause)

Name: _____   Date: _____

ASSIGNMENT: Restrictive & Non-Restrictive Clauses

In the following sentences, supply any necessary commas. If you find a comma used incorrectly, cross it out. If a sentence is correct as it is, write the letter "C" in the space at the left.

1. _____ Laurie showed the strange map to her mother who was a librarian.

2. _____ Laurie's mother worked at the Madison Public Library, which was the oldest building in town.

3. _____ Kevin was uncomfortable around people who talked constantly.

4. _____ Any book that was borrowed from Madison Library, had to be returned in three weeks.

5. _____ Laurie wanted to borrow a book that was entitled *Pirate's Treasure.*

6. _____ *Pirate's Treasure,* which contained an important clue to the mystery, had been stolen from Madison Library.

7. _____ Kevin decided to call his oldest brother who was a computer specialist.

8. _____ Summer Cove, which was Kevin's hometown, was a place, where there were many legends about pirates.

9. _____ Everyone who heard the pirate stories was fascinated by them.

10. _____ The Summer Cove Police discovered the burglar's fingerprints, which were all over the copier.

11. _____ When the Chief of Police a man named Bob Brugger got the lab results back he gave them to his top detective Sue Jamison.

12. _____ Detective Jamison interviewed library patrons, who all had library cards.

13. _____ She also began taking fingerprints which was standard procedure.

14. _____ Then the police department, which is located downtown received an anonymous tip.

15. _____ The thief was Timothy Barden who owned the local gift store, Pirate's Cove.

Critical Thinking: What kind of map do you suppose Laurie and Kevin found? Is it a pirate's map, or could it be something else? Why are Laurie and Kevin unable to read the map? Explain your answer.

PART THREE: CLAUSES

16. Noun Clauses

A **noun clause** can serve as a subject, direct object, subjective complement, or an object of a preposition—in other words, a noun clause can do anything that a noun or pronoun can do. Noun clauses are usually introduced by **subordinating words** such as *who, whom, that, what, which, whoever, whatever, whichever, when, where, why,* and *how.*

PUBLIC LIBRARY
Notices

Summer Book Club
9-11 am
June 10
July 6
August 11

Reward: Stolen Book

Reward for information leading to the arrest of the person responsible for the disappearance of Treasure Island, (rare first edition) around April of this year. Please see head librarian for details.

Book Sale:
June 30
8-12

Whoever stole the library book *should return it.*
    (noun clause as subject)

Kevin knew where the lost map was hidden.
    (direct object—most common use)

My excuse is that the dog ate my computer
    discs. (subjective complement)

I will work with whomever needs my help the
    most.
    (object of preposition)

The subordinating word often serves an important function within the noun clause. For example, in the clause *Whoever stole the library book,* the verb is *stole* and the subject of the verb is *Whoever.*

Sometimes the word *that* can be omitted from a noun clause, especially if the tone is light or informal. For example, the sentence "I know that you are lying" can also be written as "I know you're lying."

We have already learned about the **simple sentence,** which consists of one independent clause, and the **compound sentence,** which contains two or more independent clauses. There is also the **complex sentence,** which contains one independent and one dependent clause. Grammarians also speak of the **compound-complex sentence,** which contains at least two independent clauses and at least one dependent clause.

Writing Tip: Contractions, such as *you're* for *you are,* are best left to informal or personal writing. Avoid contractions in reports and essays.

Kevin lit the lantern. (simple sentence)

Kevin lit the lantern, and Laurie unfolded the map. (compound sentence)

Laurie unfolded the map, which was yellow with age. (complex sentence)

Kevin lit the lantern, and Laurie unfolded the map, which was yellow with age. (compound-complex sentence)

If you understand the different elements of a sentence—words, phrases, and clauses—you can create any kind of sentence you like, from the most simple:

Dogs barked.

to the highly elaborate, with many phrases and clauses:

As Kevin and Laurie listened in fear, they heard the sound of barking dogs, and the noise was growing louder with every passing second, as if a large pack of Dobermans and wolves was galloping through the woods with astonishing speed, prepared to devour any warm-blooded creature in its path.

If you want to be a good writer: In writing, the old saying holds true: *Variety is the spice of life.* A writer's goal should be a pleasant and interesting variety of sentences: some long, some short, many of average length, some simple, some complicated, with an occasional question or exclamation for added interest.

Kevin opened the door of the shack and went inside, and Laurie followed him. They looked around. The shack was dark and cold, and everything was covered with dust. Kevin tried not to sneeze in the musty air. Laurie shivered as a spider crawled across the ceiling. Was it a poisonous spider? As the wind whistled around the old shack, the window panes shook and rattled, and the noise mingled eerily with the distant howling of a dog. Or maybe the dog was really a wolf. How lonely the creature sounded!

Name: _____ Date: _____

ASSIGNMENT: Working With Types of Sentences

Writing Prompt: Explain what you do in a typical day on the lines below. Use as many different types of sentences as possible: long, short, medium-sized, compound, complex, and so on. Be sure to use commas correctly.

_____

_____

_____

_____

_____

_____

_____

_____

_____

_____

_____

_____

_____

_____

_____

_____

_____

_____

_____

_____

_____

_____

_____

PART FOUR: PUNCTUATION

17. The Comma and Beyond

Punctuation marks are the traffic signs of prose: they warn the reader when to slow down, when to come to a complete stop, and when to watch for something interesting or dangerous ahead. Without punctuation marks and other devices such as indentation and capitalization, most books would be difficult to read, if not impossible. Here, for example, are the opening lines of a short story:

i came as soon as i could your majesty said detective trilby to the king she scratched her bloodhounds ear whuff the bloodhound sneezed the king did not get sneezed on because he was out of range he was hanging in mid air upside down the royal magician was turning pages in the book of spells trying to find a way to help the king

This passage is much easier to read when the proper punctuation is added:

"I came as soon as I could, Your Majesty," said Detective Trilby to the king. She scratched her bloodhound's ear. "WHUFF!" the bloodhound sneezed.

The king did not get sneezed on because he was out of range. He was hanging in mid-air, upside down. The royal magician was turning pages in The Book of Spells, *trying to find a way to help the king.*

The **comma** is fairly weak. Periods, colons, semicolons, dashes, and parentheses are all stronger than commas. Nevertheless, a reader of English prose will find commas everywhere. They are used to separate words, phrases, and clauses from one another, and their purpose is to make prose easier to read.

> **Writing Tip:** Commas in a sentence function in the way pauses work when reading out loud.

We have already seen several important uses for commas. Here are a few more things to remember about them:

Use a comma to separate coordinate adjectives. Occasionally a noun will have two or three adjectives in front of it. If those adjectives are equal in importance—that is, if they are **coordinate**—they should be separated by commas.

Detective Trilby scratched the dog's soft, floppy ears.
It was a dark, blustery, gloomy night.

Occasionally, however, adjectives will form a cluster in which some words have more strength than others. Such adjectives should not be separated by commas.

Here are my red satin ballet slippers.
The conductor has a new music stand.

Sometimes it is difficult to tell whether adjectives are coordinate or not. If you are in doubt, try these simple tests:

1. Try inserting the word *and* between the adjectives. If the sentence still makes sense or sounds natural, the adjectives are coordinate.

    Detective Trilby scratched the dog's soft and floppy ears.
    Here are my red and satin and ballet slippers.

2. Try rearranging the adjectives. If the sentence still makes sense or sounds natural, the adjectives are coordinate.

    Detective Trilby scratched the dog's floppy, soft ears.
    Here are my ballet, satin, red slippers.

Adjectives of size and age are usually not separated by commas: for example, *My teacher is a little old lady.*

Use a comma to set off non-restrictive appositives. An **appositive** is a noun that renames another noun and gives additional information. It is something like a shortened adjective clause. Most appositives are non-restrictive.

Herbert Throckmorton, a man of few words, made a good impression.
    (Note the similarity to an adjective clause: *Herbert Throckmorton, who is a man of few words, made a good impression.*)
The dog, a friendly bloodhound, suffered from allergies.

Use a comma to set off parenthetical expressions—that is, words and phrases that are loosely connected with the main part of a sentence.

This secret formula, in my opinion, can save the world.
Some scientific discoveries, on the other hand, turn out to be useless.
Today is Friday, isn't it?

Years and names of states are usually considered parenthetical: *Fayetteville, Arkansas, is my home town, and July 25, 1944, is my birthday.* You should also remember to set off the so-called **nouns of direct address.**

Look at me, Jessica, and tell me the truth.   *Hail, Caesar!*
I came as soon as I could, Your Majesty.   *Houston, we have a problem.*
Look, stupid, I can't wait all day.   *Good luck, pal.*

You can also use a comma to separate words that might mistakenly be read together, as in this sentence: *While we were shooting, the principal stopped by the archery range to watch us practice.* One final word: **Don't use a lot of unnecessary commas.** They will just clutter up your pages.

Name: _____   Date: _____

ASSIGNMENT: Using Commas

Add any necessary commas to the following sentences:

1. Scott wanted to act in the school play but he had a soft voice.

2. When he got up on the stage and read for the part of Ebeneezer Scrooge no one in the back rows could understand his words.

3. Ebeneezer Scrooge has to speak in a loud gruff voice.

4. If an actor wants to be convincing as Ebeneezer Scrooge he must be forceful imaginative and dramatic.

5. Some people of course have little talent for acting.

6. Feeling disappointed because of his failure to win even a small part in *A Christmas Carol* Scott went home heaved a sigh and collapsed in front of the television set.

7. Scott's mother who was an electrician told him to try out for the lighting crew.

8. *A Christmas Carol* which is based on a book by Charles Dickens requires a lot of special lighting effects.

9. Scott knew all about electrical wiring so the director appointed him head of the lighting crew.

10. Scott who was very creative made an excellent addition to the crew and he was often asked to solve some of the most difficult lighting problems.

11. *A Christmas Carol* was a big success and when Scott didn't get a part in the next play he wasn't very disappointed.

12. He remained head of the lighting crew for the entire school year.

13. Even though he did not appear in a single play Scott was chosen as the Outstanding Theatre Student of the year.

14. Everyone loved his work and he decided that next year he would remain head of the lighting crew and only take small parts if he was needed instead of hoping for a major part in a play and not getting to work with the lighting.

BRAIN WORK: It takes more than actors to produce a play. What different kinds of work must be done around a theatre before a play can be performed?

PART FOUR: PUNCTUATION

18. Periods, Semicolons, and Colons

The **period** is used at the end of all declarative sentences and most imperative sentences. (Don't forget about the **question mark,** which is used to end interrogative sentences, and the **exclamation point,** used at the end of exclamatory sentences.)

The period is also used with abbreviations, such as *Dr.* for *Doctor, Mr.* for *Mister, Jr.* for *Junior, St.* for *Street,* and *Ave.* for *Avenue.* We will learn more about abbreviations in a later chapter.

We have already learned how to use a conjunction to join two independent clauses together to form a compound sentence.

The dog barked, and a werewolf howled in reply.

If you want to indicate that the two events—the dog's bark and the werewolf's howl—were closely related, you can join the two clauses together with a **semicolon** instead of a conjunction.

The dog barked; a werewolf howled in reply.

The semicolon has only one other use. Once in a great while, it is used to separate the items in a series—but only if some of those items contain commas of their own:

The Halloween parade consisted of Count Dracula, a vampire, Scary Hairy, a werewolf, Misty, a forlorn ghost, Caliban, a sea monster, and ten aliens from outer space.

A reader might easily get confused about how many monsters were in the parade and how many of the monsters had names. Semicolons will make this sentence easier to read:

The Halloween parade consisted of Count Dracula, a vampire; Scary Hairy, a werewolf; Misty, a forlorn ghost; Caliban, a sea monster; and ten aliens from outer space.

The **colon** is a fancy mark of punctuation for use in special situations such as business letters and important research projects. Its meaning is *Look ahead!* The colon always indicates that some kind of explanation or important material is coming up.

> **Writing Tip:** Commas and semicolons are two kinds of punctuation that can join two clauses in a complete sentence.

> *To perform this experiment, I will need the following items: a box of salt, a ball of string, a bottle of vegetable oil, a large mixing bowl, and a phial of bat's blood.*

A colon can also be used in a compound sentence if the second clause explains the first.

> *Two things happened almost at once: a dog barked, and a werewolf howled in reply.*

In a formal letter or business letter, the colon follows the salutation. For example, if you wanted to write a letter to Theodore Roosevelt, you would begin:

> *Dear President Roosevelt:*

For a friendly letter, follow the salutation with a comma:

> *Dear Teddy,*

Colons are also used to indicate the time of day (7:15 A.M.) and to separate a title from a subtitle (as in *Hercules: The Strongest Man in History*). Finally, colons are often used to introduce long quotations in research papers. As you can see, the colon is a useful device, but be careful with it. Never use a colon in the middle of an independent clause. In other words, don't use a colon between a subject and a verb, between a verb and a direct object, between a preposition and an object, or between a linking verb and a subjective complement—not even when the object or complement happens to be a series.

> **Wrong:** *To perform this experiment, I will need: a box of salt, a ball of string, a bottle of vegetable oil, a large mixing bowl, and a phial of bat's blood.*

Name: _____   Date: _____

ASSIGNMENT: Working With Punctuation Marks

How many punctuation mistakes can you find in the following letter? Rewrite the letter below, inserting the correct punctuation and deleting incorrect punctuation as needed.

Dear Mr Sterling Noble

    Last night I read in the newspaper, that you are planning to direct a major motion picture entitled *Hercules: The Strongest Man in History.* I am qualified to play Hercules for the following reasons, my strength; my acting ability; and my handsome face

    Everyone, who knows me, agrees that I am strong. I get up at 4;00 every morning to jog and lift weights. I follow my exercise period with a big breakfast of: bran muffins fat-free sausage low-calorie pancakes wheat cereal and skim milk. I pick up every heavy object in sight. People are always asking me, to carry groceries and move furniture for them.

    I am also a good actor. When I was a tiny baby only two days old I played the role of the Baby New Year in a pageant and I have been acting ever since. I can play: heroes, villains, and ordinary people. I have played a tree in *The Wizard of Oz,* a windmill in *Don Quixote,* and a clock in *Cinderella.* As for my face, you can see that I am handsome; all you have to do is look at the enclosed photograph. Everyone tells me that I am the handsomest young man in Little Illinois which is my hometown. I know you'll agree Mr Noble that you need me to play Hercules. When can I come to Hollywood for an audition!

Sincerely yours,

Buffalo Brutus

_____

_____

_____

_____

_____

_____

_____

_____

_____

_____

_____

_____

_____

_____

_____

_____

_____

PART FOUR: PUNCTUATION

19. Parentheses, Dashes, and Italics

If a parenthetical expression has no relationship whatsoever to the rest of the sentence, a pair of commas will be too weak to set it off properly. You will have to use something stronger—either **parentheses** or **dashes.** Parentheses always come in pairs. They are stronger than commas but weaker than dashes.

> *Herbert Throckmorton (I think you met him once) is a man of few words.*

In the sentence above, the clause *"I think you met him once"* has no grammatical connection to the rest of the sentence. It is not any kind of noun or verb phrase, and it is not modifying anything. It is simply "thrown in." A pair of parentheses can set it off nicely; so can a pair of dashes.

> *Herbert Throckmorton—I think you met him once—is a man of few words.*

Dashes are more informal that parentheses; they are also more emphatic. Parentheses often give the impression of enclosing a bit of information that is not particularly important. Your choice of dashes or parentheses will depend on how much emphasis you want to give to the parenthetical expression.

Writing Tip: Do not use dashes in place of commas.

> *Herbert Throckmorton (you've met him, haven't you?) is a man of few words.*
> *Herbert Throckmorton—he's such a strong, silent type!—will be the new coach.*

Sometimes a non-restrictive modifier contains commas of its own. In such a case, to avoid confusing your readers, you can set off the modifier with dashes or parentheses.

> *Herbert Throckmorton—who is a strong, silent, dignified man—will be the new coach.*
> *Some courses (for example, history, literature, and civics) require a great deal of reading and writing.*

Parentheses can also be used to enclose numbers or letters in a series.

> *I have decided not to buy the bicycle because (1) it is too expensive, (2) it is in poor condition, and (3) I don't trust the salesman, Al Oilsworth.*

A dash can be used to show an abrupt change of subject or a hesitation in a speaker's voice.

> *I said—I said—oh, nobody cares what I said!*
> *I must have made the magic spell too strong—and done it backwards!*

In informal writing, a dash can also be used like a colon, to indicate that an explanation lies ahead.

> *To perform this experiment, I will need the following items—a box of salt, a ball of string, a bottle of vegetable oil, a large mixing bowl, and a phial of bat's blood.*

Because the dash has so many uses, some writers enjoy scattering dashes everywhere. Such a practice may be fine for friendly letters, because dashes can make a letter seem lively and personal. But a dash is a strong, emphatic mark; and, like any such device, it must be used with care. Except in friendly letters, too many dashes will give your writing a nervous, scatterbrained, or hysterical quality. (Of course, if you are writing a story about a character who really is nervous, scatterbrained, and hysterical, you can feel free to use a lot of dashes whenever he or she starts to talk.)

A simple way to emphasize a word or phrase is to use **italics.** Many computers can print italic script, but if you are writing by hand, underlining serves the same purpose as italics.

> It's not a dog in the back yard, Laurie; it's a *werewolf!*
> Help! There's a <u>werewolf</u> in the yard!

Like the dash, this device should be used sparingly. Italics can also be used to indicate words used as words.

> The word *education* is difficult to define.
> Commander Lovell did not know the meaning of the word <u>fear</u>.

Italics should also be used for titles of long literary and artistic works, such as books, full-length movies, two- or three-act plays, television series, magazines, and newspapers.

Adventures of Huckleberry Finn	<u>Time</u>
The Phantom of the Opera	<u>Apollo 13</u>
<u>Chicago Tribune</u>	*Star Trek*

Writing Tip: You must use italics or underlining when writing a bibliography. Make sure you know which parts of a citation to italicize or underline.

Name: _____ Date: _____

PERFORMANCE TASK: Answering a Letter

Writing Prompt: *You are Mr. Sterling Noble, famous Hollywood director. On the lines below, answer the letter from Buffalo Brutus that appears in Chapter 18. You should thank Mr. Brutus for offering to audition for the leading role in the film* Hercules: The Strongest Man in History. *Then, as politely as possible, explain to Mr. Brutus that you have already cast a major Hollywood star as Hercules. Wish Mr. Brutus good luck in his acting career, and suggest that he might try an audition at the Little Community Theatre. Suggest some roles that he might play.* Hint: *Remember that this is a business letter, not a friendly letter.*

_____

_____

_____

_____

_____

_____

_____

_____

_____

_____

_____

_____

_____

_____

_____

_____

_____

_____

_____

_____

_____

_____

_____

PART FOUR: PUNCTUATION

20. That Pesky Apostrophe

The apostrophe is the pest among punctuation marks. It is the device that everyone either forgets or misuses. However, a student who wishes to be a good writer must learn how to use it correctly. The apostrophe has two main uses.

1. **Use an apostrophe to show possession** (that is, to form the **possessive case**)

    a. Add an apostrophe and an -*s* to form the possessive case of a singular noun:

       the boy's house   the child's mother

    b. When a plural noun ends in -*s,* use an apostrophe to form the possessive case:

       the boys' homes   the players' locker room

    c. When a plural noun does not end in -*s,* use an apostrophe followed by an -*s* to form the possessive case:

       the men's lockers   the children's room

    d. On those rare occasions when a singular noun ends in -*s,* you have a choice: to form the possessive case, use either an apostrophe alone or an apostrophe followed by an -*s.* Experts disagree on which method is better, so ask your teacher which method he or she prefers:

    > **WritingTip:** You can also use the apostrophe to form the plurals of letters, as in *I got three A's on my report card.*

       the duchess' gown or the duchess's gown
       Prince Charles' castle or Prince Charles's castle

Whichever you choose, be consistent. If you are writing a report about Prince Charles, don't begin with *Charles' castle* and end with *Charles's castle.*

Note: Never use an apostrophe to change a singular noun to the plural form.

Wrong: *The three boy's enjoyed watching movie's.*

e. Use an apostrophe and an *-s* for the possessive form of indefinite pronouns:

everyone's friend   nobody's friend

As usual, the personal pronouns have to be different. None of them uses an apostrophe to form the possessive case.

	SINGULAR	PLURAL
First person	my, mine	our, ours
Second person	your, yours	your, yours
Third person	his, her, hers, its, whose	their, theirs, whose

2. **Use an apostrophe in contractions.** A **contraction** combines two or more words into one, with a letter or letters missing. Use an apostrophe in place of the missing material:

does not = doesn't   let us = let's
of the clock = o'clock   they are = they're

Unfortunately, some of the most popular contractions sound exactly like the possessive forms of some personal pronouns. Remember that a personal pronoun has no apostrophe.

CONTRACTION	PERSONAL PRONOUN
it is = it's	its
you are = you're	your
they are = they're	their
who is = who's	whose
there is = there's	theirs

From these examples, you can see why the apostrophe is a pest.

Name: _____ Date: _____

ASSIGNMENT: The Apostrophe & Other Punctuation

Correct the punctuation in the following sentences. If a sentence is correct as it is, write the letter "C" in the space at the left.

1. _____ Dont tell me about you're problem's because Im tired of listening.

2. _____ The police cant find out who's responsible for stealing Coach Wilsons wallet.

3. _____ Beth's kitten has hurt it's paw so we'll take it to the veterinarian's clinic.

4. _____ John; havent you finished feeding the horse's yet.

5. _____ Let's borrow Amys bicycle, go to the store, and buy: cookies, popcorn, and candy.

6. _____ The womens' basketball team has won all of they're games this season.

7. _____ Cant you figure out what the problem is;

8. _____ Why don't you finish your homework, and then we'll go out for pizza?

9. _____ Their going to raise the price of football tickets this season; now, there going to cost a fortune?

10. _____ Look Leslie its not going to happen so stop asking about it!

11. _____ Who's bike is parked in the middle of the living room?

12. _____ It feels like it's been years since Spring Break, but it's only been three weeks!

13. _____ I can't figure out this math problem; I don't know who can.

14. _____ Harry told me to—wait; dont you want to know what he said.

15. _____ I can't believe I forgot to study for the test: now Im going to fail!

16. _____ My moms so mean, she wont buy me that new game system.

17. _____ I'd love to go out for ice cream, but let me check my calendar first.

18. _____ I wont be at the basketball game tonight; because Ive got to go visit my grand-mother.

19. _____ The princesss gown was long and blue and covered with tiny pearls.

20. _____ I dont just believe in ghosts; Ive <u>seen</u> one.

PART FOUR: PUNCTUATION

21. Quotation Marks

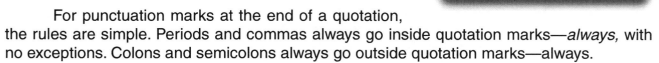

Quotation marks always appear in pairs. Their main use is to enclose **direct quotations**—the exact words of a speaker or writer. Expressions such as *he said* and *she shouted* are set off by commas.

> *"I came as soon as I could," said Detective Trilby to the king.*
> *Detective Trilby said, "I came as soon as I could."*
> *"As you can see," said the king, "something has gone wrong with our magic."*

For punctuation marks at the end of a quotation, the rules are simple. Periods and commas always go inside quotation marks—*always,* with no exceptions. Colons and semicolons always go outside quotation marks—always.

> *"And now, Delbert," Coach Wilson said, "sit up and listen to me."*
> *Coach Wilson said, "Delbert, listen to me"; Delbert, however, paid no attention.*
> *Dr. Van Helsing said that he would need "a few common household items": a box of salt, a ball of string, a bottle of vegetable oil, a large mixing bowl, and a phial of bat's blood.*

Writing Tip: Before quoting a person, attach a comma to *said*, as in *Coach Wilson said, "sit up and listen."*

Exclamation points and question marks usually go inside quotation marks. Occasionally, however, a question mark belongs to the main part of the sentence, not the quotation. On such occasions, the question mark should be placed *outside* the quotation marks: *Did Benjamin Franklin really say, "Fish and guests begin to smell after three days"?*

The so-called **indirect quotation** reports what a speaker said but does not use his exact words. An indirect quotation is not a true quotation, however, and should not be enclosed in quotation marks.

> **Direct quotation:** *John said, "Jennifer, will you marry me?"* (John's exact words)
> **Indirect quotation:** *John asked Jennifer whether she would marry him.*
> (*Not* John's exact words—no quotation marks needed)

Notice that the second example contains an **indirect question** as well as an indirect quotation. No question mark is needed because the sentence is phrased as a statement.

Quotation marks are also used to enclose titles of *short* works—short stories, articles, songs, one-act plays, chapters, short poems, and single episodes of television series. You will remember that italics or underlining is used for titles of long works:

> The most famous episode of *Star Trek* was called "The Trouble with Tribbles."
> In *The Sound of Music,* Julie Andrews sang "My Favorite Things."

Name: _____   Date: _____

ASSIGNMENT: Using Punctuation Marks

Read the following short story carefully, taking note of how punctuation marks are used. Notice that a new paragraph begins with every change of speaker.

Topsy-Turvy

"I came as soon as I could, Your Majesty," said Detective Trilby to the king. She scratched her bloodhound's ear. "WHUFF!" the bloodhound sneezed.

The king did not get sneezed on because he was out of range. He was hanging in mid-air, upside down. The royal magician was turning pages in *The Book of Spells,* trying to find a way to help the king. He had tied himself to a heavy chair to keep from floating away. His young assistant helped him hold the book steady.

Dishes, books, umbrellas, and musical instruments floated around the room, all of them upside down. The royal band leader was hanging by his knees from the chandelier, trying to catch a trumpet that floated just beyond his reach.

"Quick, Detective, grab hold of the banister before you float away!" said the magician. Detective Trilby held onto the banister with one hand and seized the bloodhound's collar with the other hand. "SNORFF!" sneezed the bloodhound.

"As you can see, something has gone terribly wrong with our magic," said the king, speaking as well as a man can speak when he is hanging upside down. "Yesterday everyone turned invisible. We had to wear sheets to keep from bumping into one another. The day before that, it was a sleeping spell—which was good for me, at least, because I've always been a light sleeper—but it was terrible for the royal band leader. He started snoring in the middle of a concert! And today everything is topsy-turvy!"

"Some evil wizard has put a curse on this castle!" said the band leader, swinging on the chandelier and snatching up a pair of flutes.

"Have you actually seen an evil wizard lurking around?" Detective Trilby asked.

"No," said the band leader as he neatly caught a flying clarinet, "but what does that prove? Evil wizards can make themselves invisible."

"PFOOF!" The bloodhound sneezed so hard that the chandelier rattled and shook, sending the royal band leader and his instruments flying.

"The poor dog!" said the magician's assistant. He stroked the bloodhound's soft, floppy ears. "Does he always sneeze like that?"

"Yes," said Detective Trilby. "He has allergies."

"But what's the use of a bloodhound if he can't smell?" asked the royal magician.

"No use," said Detective Trilby. "But he's a good friend."

*****

Around midnight, the magician finally found a way to break the topsy-turvy spell. Detective Trilby went to her room, but instead of going to sleep, she sat awake in bed, waiting to see whether anything strange would happen.

Suddenly the bloodhound began to sneeze furiously. So did Detective Trilby. "Ah-choo! Ah-choo!" she gasped. "Good heavens! Maybe there really *is* an evil wizard loose in the castle."

Name: _____ Date: _____

Then something even stranger happened. The vase of flowers on her night stand began to overflow with water. Detective Trilby sprang out of bed with a splash and found herself standing in water up to her ankles.

The king ran into the room. He was weeping and wringing out his handkerchief. "I can't stop crying!" he sobbed. "The fish pond and the moat are overflowing, and every faucet in the castle is pouring out water. We'll all drown!"

They splashed their way to the magician's laboratory. The royal magician was crying, sneezing, and shouting at his assistant, all at the same time. "Ah-choo! Get me *The Book of Spells* (sob, sob). Turn to the chapter on plumbing and read it to me. Oh, boo-hoo-HOO!"

The assistant grabbed *The Book of Spells,* which was about to float out the door and into the moat. He turned to a chapter entitled "How to Un-Hex Your Plumbing" and read aloud: "You need a bag of desert wind, ten pounds of cactus leaves, and a book of the world's dullest, driest speeches."

The magician had to read the dull speeches for three hours until everyone was worn out. The band leader summoned his musicians and directed a concert of the most boring marches ever written. At last the castle was dry, and everyone had stopped sneezing and weeping.

"Well, another day, another evil spell," said the king. "I can't live like this much longer. Maybe I should retire to a desert island."

"That won't be necessary," Detective Trilby said. "I know who's been causing all the trouble, and it isn't an evil wizard."

"Then who?" asked the magician's assistant.

"I mean *you,* young man," said Detective Trilby. "You're the only one who wasn't sneezing tonight or floating away yesterday. You've been practicing your master's spells, haven't you?"

The assistant burst into tears—real tears this time, straight from the heart. "I was only trying to help the king," he sobbed. "His Majesty was having trouble sleeping, and I always wanted to be a magician. But my sleeping spell put everyone to sleep, not just the king—and then all of the magic went out of control. Last night I tried to make a little spell for dryness, to cure your poor dog's runny nose, but I must have made the spell too strong—and done it backwards!"

The magician's face was red with anger. "You're a menace in the laboratory!" he shouted. "You're fired!"

"Not so fast," said the king. "This boy has a kind heart and a real flair for powerful spells. Sir Magician, you could teach him to be the greatest wizard in the country—and you'd become famous as the world's greatest teacher."

The magician's snarl turned into a beaming smile. "I always *did* want to go down in history," he said. "Detective Trilby, we're so grateful to you."

"And I'm grateful to you, too," she said. "Haven't you noticed that my dog has stopped sneezing? His allergy is cured."

"Woof," said the bloodhound dryly.

Critical Thinking: The royal band leader is quick to blame the king's problem on an evil wizard, even though no one has seen such a person lurking about. Have you ever known anyone who was quick to leap to conclusions without any evidence? Give specific details or examples to support your answer.

Name: _____ Date: _____

ASSIGNMENT: Working With Quotation Marks

Writing Prompt: *Complete the following conversation, being careful to use punctuation marks correctly.*

   "Jake, what's that noise?" Sarah asked her brother.
   "I don't hear anything," said Jake, barely looking up from his copy of *Chemistry Made Simple.* "What noise?"
   "That scratching sound. It seems to be coming from the attic."
   "Probably just the wind."
   "Jake, will you put down that book and listen? There isn't any wind tonight. I sure do wish Mom and Dad were home."

_____

_____

_____

_____

_____

_____

_____

_____

_____

_____

_____

_____

_____

_____

_____

_____

_____

_____

PART FOUR: PUNCTUATION

22. Abbreviations

An **abbreviation** is a shortened form of a word or words, such as *Dr.* for *Doctor*, *Blvd.* for *Boulevard*, and *NASA* for *National Aeronautics and Space Administration*. As you can see from these examples, some abbreviations require periods and some do not. A few abbreviations are acceptable in formal writing, but most are not.

When an abbreviation is used as part of a person's name, it is probably acceptable in any sort of writing:

> Mr. and Mrs. Jones   Dr. Jason Jones
> Jason Jones Jr.   Jessica Jones, Ph.D.

Abbreviated names of streets and states may be used in addresses but should be spelled out in formal writing. In formal writing, abbreviations should be kept to a minimum.

> **Writing Tip:** The word *Miss* is not an abbreviation and needs no period. The title *Ms.* can be used either with or without a period.

> **Poor:** *My Dr. has an office on Madison St. in Peoria, Ill. Every Sept. he goes to NYC w/ his assistant to study & do research.*

> **Better:** *My doctor has an office on Madison Street in Peoria, Illinois. Every September he goes to New York City with his assistant to study and do research.*

Suppose you want to write about an organization or a process with a fifteen-syllable name. Do you have to keep writing this huge name over and over? Not necessarily. The best way to avoid confusing a reader is to write the complete name out once, follow it with the abbreviation in parentheses, and then use the abbreviation in the rest of your paper:

> Last week the Good News Club of Little listened to a speech by Jim Davis, the president of Quality Unlimited Advisory Council for Kids (QUACK). Davis explained why QUACK is disgusted by most Saturday morning cartoon shows. . . .

The U.S. Postal Service prefers periods and other punctuation be omitted from addresses on envelopes. The two-letter abbreviations of states: AL for Alabama, AK for Alaska, and so on, are always capitalized and used with ZIP codes. They require no periods.

Abbreviations of technical terms, government agencies, and organizations are often capitalized and require no periods. Familiar examples are *DVD* (digital video disc), *DWI* (driving while intoxicated), and *FBI* (Federal Bureau of Investigation). If you are in doubt about whether an abbreviation requires periods or not, check your dictionary—but don't be surprised to find that dictionaries sometimes disagree with one another.

Name: _____ Date: _____

ASSIGNMENT: Punctuation

Rewrite the following sentences to correct the punctuation.

1. Detective Trilby asked the band leader, "whether he had ever seen an evil wizard in the castle." _____

   _____

2. Detective Trilby a clever woman said to the king, "I know whose responsible for the evil spells." _____

   _____

3. The fish pond, and the moat were overflowing; and the faucets were pouring water into the castle. _____

   _____

4. Darcy Andrews lived in Little Ill. but her dream was to work for N.A.S.A.

   _____

5. "Miss. Andrews", said the teacher, "come down from outer space and stop dreaming about satellite's and rocket's". _____

   _____

6. Darcy lived across the st. from Mr. Porters neighborhood grocery store _____

   _____

7. Mr Porter, who believed in flying saucers gave some of his old science fiction magazines to Darcy. _____

   _____

8. One bright day in Oct. Darcy went to the store; to buy a loaf of bread and found Mr Porter hiding under the counter. _____

   _____

9. "Hide quick"! he whispered to Darcy "I just saw an alien from outer space." _____

   _____

10. Are you sure it wasnt a child in a Halloween costume," Darcy asked? _____

   _____

Final note on punctuation: By now you can probably see that punctuation is more than just a list of "rules" to be learned or memorized. A writer builds with words, phrases, and clauses, but he needs punctuation marks to guide his readers. Hence, punctuation marks are not separate from meaning; they are part of the meaning of any piece of written work.

PART FIVE: MAJOR SENTENCE ERRORS

23. The Sentence Fragment

A writer can forget a comma once in a while without doing any serious harm to his written work. However, some grammatical mistakes are so obvious that any educated reader will notice them immediately. Such an error is the **sentence fragment,** which is exactly what its name says it is—an incomplete piece of a sentence. There are many kinds of sentence fragments, but the most common types are a dependent clause or verbal phrase punctuated as if it were an independent clause.

I refuse to vote for Senator Foghorn. Because he never keeps his promises.
I have one goal for this year. To make the team.

Sometimes the second part of a compound verb gets mistaken for a sentence.

Cautiously Darcy peered into the dark basement. But saw nothing unusual
Tonight I have to write a book report. And study for my history test.

A fragment might be a noun followed by an adjective clause.

I refuse to vote for Senator Foghorn. A man who never keeps his promises.

The usual cure for a sentence fragment is to attach it to a complete sentence.

I refuse to vote for Senator Foghorn because he never keeps his promises.
I have one major goal for this year—to make the soccer team.

You might also rewrite the fragment as a complete sentence.

I refuse to vote for Senator Foghorn. He never keeps his promises.
Cautiously Darcy peered into the dark basement. She saw nothing unusual.

Sometimes an imperative sentence is mistaken for a fragment because such a sentence appears to have no subject. This appearance is deceiving. Grammarians say that the subject of every imperative sentence is the "understood" word *you.* Thus *"Shut the door"* really means *"You shut the door."*

A writer who cannot tell a sentence from a fragment is in trouble, because a sentence is a basic unit of composition. Nevertheless, fragments are sometimes useful. When fictional characters talk to each other, fragments often turn up in their conversation: *"Another day, another evil spell," said the king.*

Like any literary device, the fragment must be used sparingly, if at all.

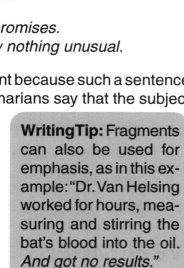

WritingTip: Fragments can also be used for emphasis, as in this example: "Dr. Van Helsing worked for hours, measuring and stirring the bat's blood into the oil. *And got no results."*

Name: _____ Date: _____

ASSIGNMENT: Sentence Fragments

Read each of the following sentences carefully. If you find mistakes, revise and improve the sentence. If you find no mistakes, write Correct on the blank.

1. I plan to go to the Singing Zombies concert. If I can convince Mom to buy me a ticket. _____

   _____

2. I can't stand Delbert. He never stops talking about himself. _____

   _____

3. Please hand me a knife and some plates. I want to cut the birthday cake. _____

   _____

4. Jason is a good actor. Who practices in front of a mirror until he can speak his lines per-

   fectly. _____

   _____

5. Alice searched all morning and afternoon. But couldn't find the lost puppy. _____

   _____

6. Alice was starting to grow discouraged. But she refused to give up. _____

   _____

7. Darcy wandered through the dark woods. Growing more frightened every minute.

   _____

8. This week our soccer team plays the Quincy Panthers. A team that is almost impossible

   to beat. _____

   _____

9. The Panthers' mascot is Norbert Swizzle. Who dresses like a giant black cat and dances

   the Charleston while twirling a baton. _____

   _____

10. During the summer Norbert works at a zoo. He knows how a panther behaves.

   _____

PART FIVE: MAJOR SENTENCE ERRORS

24. The Comma Splice and the Run-On Sentence

Suppose you want to join two sentences together to form a compound sentence, as in:

> *Count Dracula had to stay out of the sunlight. He also had to avoid mirrors, garlic, and silver bullets.*

There are several ways of joining these sentences together. You might use a coordinating conjunction or a pair of correlative conjunctions.

> *Count Dracula had to stay out of the sunlight, and he also had to avoid mirrors, garlic, and silver bullets.*
>
> *Not only did Count Dracula have to stay out of the sunlight, but he also had to avoid mirrors, garlic, and silver bullets.*

If you want to emphasize the close relationship between the two clauses, you might use a semicolon. For different emphasis, you could revise the sentence and use a colon.

> *Count Dracula had to stay out of the sunlight; he also had to avoid mirrors, garlic, and silver bullets.*
>
> *Count Dracula had several problems: he had to avoid sunlight, mirrors, garlic, and silver bullets.*

However, **you can't use a comma to join independent clauses.** A comma is a weak mark of punctuation. It is used to separate things, not join them together.

> **Wrong:** *Count Dracula had to stay out of the sunlight, he also had to avoid mirrors, garlic, and silver bullets.*

Such a mistake is called a **comma splice**. Even worse is the **run-on sentence**, in which two independent clauses are run together with no punctuation at all, nothing to indicate where one clause ends and another begins. Such sentences are bewildering.

> **Writing Tip:** A run-on sentence is also known as a **fused sentence** or a **run-together sentence**.

> **Wrong:** *Count Dracula had to stay out of the sunlight he also had to avoid mirrors, garlic, and silver bullets.*

Remember your readers. Learn to construct your sentences without comma splices and run-on sentences.

Name: _____   Date: _____

ASSIGNMENT: Sentence Fragments, Comma Splices, and Run-On Sentences

Read each of the following sentences carefully. If you find mistakes, revise and improve the sentence. If you find no mistakes, write Correct on the blank.

1. Eric's house has an unusual feature there is a secret room behind the fireplace.

   _____

2. Eric and his friends have a clubhouse in the secret room, they like to meet there and play a board game called *Sword and Sorcery*. _____

   _____

3. Sometimes they also play chess and checkers. Or hold business meetings and elections.

   _____

4. Their secret password is *courage;* their mascot is a black cat. _____

   _____

5. The secret room has no electricity. But the members use candles to light their meetings.

   _____

6. Eric's house is surrounded by a stone wall and big trees. Which make the place look dark and mysterious. _____

   _____

7. The house is old. It was built before the Civil War by Eric's ancestors. _____

   _____

8. The secret room is a mystery. Because nobody knows why it was built into the house.

   _____

9. None of the family diaries or other records say anything about a secret room, Eric's great-grandmother can't explain the mystery either. _____

   _____

10. All the family knows is that the room has been a family secret the room wasn't even shown to the electrician who installed the electricity. In the house many years ago.

   _____

Critical Thinking: Can you think of some reasons for a secret room in a house that was built before the Civil War? Explain your answer.

PART FIVE: MAJOR SENTENCE ERRORS

25. Problems With Agreement

If you study the conjugations on page 12, you will notice a peculiarity about the present and present perfect tenses: third-person verbs change to show **number**—that is, singular and plural.

SINGULAR	PLURAL
He loves	They love
She has loved	They have loved

The verb *be* makes several changes to show number.

SINGULAR	PLURAL
I am	We are
You are	You are
He is	They are . . . and so forth

The passive and progressive forms also have several singular and plural forms because they are formed with the verb *be.*

I am loved	We are loved
I was going	We were going

An important rule of grammar is that the subject must **agree** with the verb. That is, if the subject is singular, the verb must be singular also; if the subject is plural, the verb must be plural.

Wrong	Right
He love his mother	He loves his mother
I is loved	I am loved
I were going home	I was going home
We has gone home.	We have gone home

A compound verb presents a problem: Does it need a singular or a plural verb? The guidelines are simple: Compound subjects joined by *and* are almost always plural and take plural verbs. If a compound subject is joined by *or,* the verb should agree with whichever subject is closer: *Joe and Kristin deliver newspapers* but *Joe or Kristin delivers newspapers* (that is, one or the other will show up with newspapers, but never both at once). *The children or their father delivers newspapers* but *The father or his children deliver newspapers.*

Sometimes a parenthetical element or a prepositional phrase appears between a subject and its verb. That element does not affect the number of the subject.

Delbert and his forty cousins come to every soccer game.

Delbert, along with his forty cousins, comes to every soccer game.

One of the forty cousins comes to every game. (*One*, not *cousins*, is the subject.)

What about such collective nouns as *class, team, jury, orchestra, audience,* and the like? Answer: A collective noun is considered singular if the members of the group are acting together; it is considered plural if the members are acting as individuals.

> **Writing Tip:** Remember, the subject must **agree** with the verb.

Our debate team wins every tournament. (Winning is a group
  effort.)

The debate team are wearing their new blazers and carrying their new briefcases.
  (It would be absurd to say "The debate team is wearing its new blazer.")

Indefinite pronouns can be confusing. Words such as *everyone, everybody, anyone, anybody, someone, somebody, no one,* and *nobody* are usually singular: *Everyone is working hard. Nobody is working hard.* Words like *some, all, several, both,* and *many* are plural: *Some are working hard. All are working hard.*

Name: _____ Date: _____

ASSIGNMENT: Subject-Verb Agreement

Read each of the following sentences carefully. If you find mistakes, revise and improve the sentence. If you find no mistakes, write Correct on the blank.

1. Jerry and Beth is working together on a school project. _____
   _____

2. They has organized an election for president of Mrs. Andrew's government class.
   _____

3. Jerry, together with a few of his classmates, is printing the ballots and preparing a list of registered voters. _____
   _____

4. Beth and her friends have contacted the school newspaper about advertising.
   _____

5. Two political parties has been formed by the class, and everyone have chosen a party to join. _____
   _____

6. One of the parties has nominated Anne Taylor to run for president. _____
   _____

7. Gerry Davies were chosen by the other party as their nominee. _____
   _____

8. Mrs. Andrews says that the entire class is working hard to make the election a success.
   _____
   _____

9. Mrs. Andrews or two students presents the latest election news every day before class starts. _____
   _____

10. Davies and Taylor was in a close race, but Taylor won. _____
    _____

PART FIVE: MAJOR SENTENCE ERRORS

26. Dangling and Misplaced Modifiers

The point of an adjective is to modify a noun or pronoun. Therefore, a writer must provide every adjective with a logical word to modify. Otherwise, the adjective will simply attach itself to the nearest noun, whether that makes sense or not. Most writers have no trouble with one-word adjectives or participles, as in:

The barking dog chased the mailman.

However, a careless writer will sometimes put a participle phrase in the wrong place.

> *Barking so loudly that he could be heard all over town, the mailman was chased by the German shepherd.*

It is good to remember this rule: If an adjective phrase is placed at the beginning of a sentence, **it must modify the subject of the sentence.** Failure to observe this rule will result in the so-called **dangling modifier.** Dangling modifiers are often ridiculous.

> *After driving to the cabin, dinner had to be prepared.* (Dinner was driving to the cabin?)
> *Pacing the floor worriedly, my telephone began to ring.* (The telephone was pacing?)
> *At the age of ten, Joe's father took him to Yellowstone Park.* (Joe's dad was ten when he took his son to Yellowstone?)

There are two ways to repair the damage of a dangling modifier. You could change the subject of the sentence:

> *After driving to the cabin, we had to prepare dinner.*
> *Pacing the floor worriedly, I heard the telephone ring.*
> *At the age of ten, Joe went to Yellowstone Park with his father.*

Writing Tip: Keep your modifiers close to your subjects.

Or you could change the adjective phrase to an adverb clause:

> *After we drove to the cabin, dinner had to be prepared.*
> *While I was pacing the floor worriedly, the telephone began to ring.*
> *When Joe was ten years old, his father took him to Yellowstone Park.*

A **misplaced modifier** is similar to the dangling modifier, except that it appears in the middle or at the end of a sentence, rather than at the beginning. Both adjectives and adverbs can be misplaced.

> **Misplaced:** *It is a poor idea to buy gifts for loyal friends that are cheap.*
> **Improved:** *It is a poor idea to buy cheap gifts for loyal friends.*

Name: _____ Date: _____

ASSIGNMENT: Dangling and Misplaced Modifiers

Revise and improve the following sentences:

1. Walking down the dusty road, a black convertible roared over the hill and almost struck me. _____
   _____

2. Sleeping peacefully, the alarm clock rang in Jenny's ear. _____
   _____

3. After eating a big Sunday dinner, a nap seemed like a good idea to me. _____
   _____

4. Stumbling sleepily into the classroom, Delbert's books dropped to the floor. _____
   _____

5. The audience cheered when Tonya finished her piano solo in the balcony. _____
   _____

6. Traveling on icy roads, serious automobile accidents can occur. _____
   _____

7. People often avoid black cats who are superstitious. _____
   _____

8. I saw Biff Williams run eighty yards for a touchdown while nibbling popcorn and watching television. _____
   _____

9. Skating perfectly, a gold medal was won by my brother at the State Winter Olympics.
   _____
   _____

10. Mother made a cake for the family that was dripping with chocolate frosting. _____
    _____

BRAINWORK: *On your own paper, write two or three absurd examples of dangling or misplaced modifiers.*

PART FIVE: MAJOR SENTENCE ERRORS

27. Shifts in Tense and Viewpoint

Unless a writer has a good reason for doing otherwise, he or she should stick to the same tense. Failure to follow this rule is known as **tense shift.**

> **Wrong:** *Cinderella went to the ball and danced with the prince until midnight. But when she hears the clock strike twelve, she runs from the ballroom and loses her glass slipper.*

> **Improved:** *Cinderella goes to the ball and dances with the prince until midnight. But when she hears the clock strike twelve, she runs from the ballroom and loses her glass slipper.*

Most writers use the present tense to report on a book or summarize the plot of a work of fiction. They use the past tense to write about history or to write stories of their own.

> *Huckleberry Finn escapes from his father and joins Jim for an adventurous journey down the Mississippi River.* (Summary of Mark Twain's famous novel—present tense. The events in *Huckleberry Finn* never change.)

> *Napoleon gained control of France and crowned himself Emperor.* (Historical events that happened, once and for all time, in the past.)

> *One bright spring morning I decided to skip school and search for an adventure. So I sneaked past the bus stop, slipped down the alleys, and wandered along the road to Dead Man's Pond.* (The author is writing a fictional story of his own.)

These traditions are not iron-clad rules; some writers use verb tenses in unusual ways—using the present tense to write a work of fiction, for example: *It is a bright spring morning. As I am eating breakfast, it occurs to me that the day is too beautiful to be wasted on school. I decide to search for adventure.* Whatever tense a writer chooses, he or she must stick with it—unless the writer is talking about events that occurred at different times: *Yesterday I washed the car, today I pack my suitcases, and tomorrow I will leave for my trip.*

> **Writing Tip:** Different styles of writing use different tenses.

A writer should also be careful not to shift **viewpoint**—that is, to shift between first, second, and third person without a good reason.

> **Wrong:** *After Cinderella married the prince, she discovered that you have to work hard to maintain a palace.*

> **Improved:** *After Cinderella married the prince, she discovered that she would have to work hard to maintain a palace.*

Name: _____   Date: _____

ASSIGNMENT: Time and Viewpoint

On your own paper, revise and improve the following passages:

1. Benjamin Franklin was a successful printer and newspaper publisher, but science gave him more pleasure than business. After he has earned enough money to live comfortably, he devotes his time to doing his famous scientific experiments with electricity.

2. Dorothy was carried away by a tornado to Munchkin land in the magical world of Oz. The Munchkins are charming and their world is beautiful, but Dorothy wants nothing more than to return to her home in Kansas. Besides, she needs to escape from a wicked witch. Accompanied by a talking scarecrow, Dorothy left the Munchkins and began her journey to find the wonderful Wizard of Oz.

3. Once upon a time there was a beautiful princess who could fly. She enjoyed flying so much that she spent all of her time soaring through the air. When she comes down to earth long enough to attend a royal ball, she looks so windblown and rumpled that nobody wants to dance with her. The king worried that his daughter would never find a husband. "Alas, alas!" he cries one day. "My beautiful daughter will die an old maid, and I'll never have grandchildren!"

4. One thing I have learned is that you have to study every day if you want to succeed in school. If a student tries to do all of his week's homework on Sunday night, you will be too tired to concentrate on Monday morning. I always study for an hour after school, and I also make good use of study hall. In this way a student can get his homework done, and you will still have time to enjoy nights and weekends.

5. I have discovered that you can be creative in some way no matter who you are. One person might be a terrific artist, another a great dancer, and someone else an inventor, but all are creative. Even if you are a chemist you can be creative in your experiments, but everyone does something creative. You may even be creative when you daydream in class!

BRAINWORK: *Even though most stories are told in past tense, a few modern writers prefer the present tense for fiction. They believe that the present tense helps a reader to become more involved in the story. On your own paper, try rewriting a well-known legend, tall tale, or fairy story using the present tense. Do you find the present tense more exciting, or do you prefer the past tense?*

PART FIVE: MAJOR SENTENCE ERRORS

28. Garbled and Confusing Sentences

The **garbled sentence** is the despair of teachers every-where. Like a three-wheeled car or a two-story house with no staircases, a garbled sentence defies the rules of logic. Modifiers stick out in all directions with nothing to modify. Verbs get lost in a swamp of words. Nothing seems to fit.

> *Malcomb, as a talented young man and showing great ability to play basketball since the second grade, the best player on the team, nevertheless got into a bitter argument which happened during the homecoming game with*
> *a referee and now may be getting suspended from the team and not, even though he has always been a model student, go to the State Tournament.*

What, if anything, can you do to prevent garbled sentences? Unfortunately, there are as many ways to garble a sentence as there are stars in the universe, so no simple set of rules exists. A good thing to keep in mind, however, is that many sentences become garbled **because they are too long.** The example above contains enough material for at least four sentences. Remember that a long sentence is not necessarily any better than a short sentence. If you need four sentences, write four sentences.

> *Malcomb was a talented young man, and ever since the second grade, he had shown great ability to play basketball. He was not only the best player on our team but also a model student. So everyone at the homecoming game was surprised when Malcomb got into a bitter argument with one of the referees. Would he be suspended from the team and forbidden to go to the State Tournament?*

Writing Tip: A sentence is not a suitcase; it need not be "packed" with everything that comes to mind.

You should avoid **split constructions.** Don't separate words that belong together. Keep subjects close to verbs, auxiliaries close to main verbs, verbs close to objects, and adjectives close to nouns. It is possible to place a short modifier between a subject and a verb: *Kevin, tired and discouraged, went home.* But avoid sentences like the following:

> *Kevin, exhausted after working all day with no time to rest and feeling that he had little left to hope for and nothing to gain by waiting any longer, went home.*

> *I have never, although I have been going to concerts all my life and have attended some pretty bad ones, heard any sound as painfully ear-splitting as Mrs. Warble's voice.*

Above all, remember that a sentence is a structure built according to logical rules. A writer can't build a good sentence by piling words on top of words, any more than a carpenter can build a house by throwing lumber, tiles, and carpets together in a heap.

Name: _____ Date: _____

ASSIGNMENT: Major Sentence Errors

Revise and improve the following passages:

1. After only two lessons I was swiftly, even though I had never tried it before and have always been a little afraid of water, skimming across the lake on my new skis. Waving at the people on the shore and enjoying the wind in your face. That day I got over my fear of water once and for all I also learned to love adventure.

    _____

    _____

    _____

    _____

    _____

2. The lamp was the ugliest thing I had ever seen in my life, it looked like a giant green amoeba with a ruffled pink lamp shade. A gift from Aunt Harriet. Searching patiently through several shops, the lamp cost her a lot of money. You always have to act happy when somebody gives you a present. So I said, "Wow, I never saw anything like this before."

    _____

    _____

    _____

    _____

    _____

3. The drama club are presenting a play about children who have been abandoned on Friday night at seven o'clock in the gymnasium. Michael and his sister has written the script, Adam will play the leading role of Sergeant Kingston who is a student in the seventh grade.

    _____

    _____

    _____

    _____

    _____

BRAINWORK: *Write something* terrible! *Dangle every modifier, split every construction, run every sentence together. Choose any subject you like, but be sure to write as badly as possible. Maybe the class can vote for the best piece of bad writing or even give an award.*

PART SIX: WRITING PROSE

29. The Importance of the Paragraph

A **paragraph,** the basic unit of prose, is the development of a single point or idea. Writers always signal the beginning of a paragraph by **indenting** the first line. The usual indentation is five spaces on a typewriter or the preset tab on the computer.

Paragraphs serve two important purposes. First, they are reassuring to the reader. Most people are intimidated by long stretches of unbroken print with no resting place in sight. It would be a scary chore to tackle a book in which each chapter was sixty pages long, with no subdivisions and no paragraphs. The average reader would throw such a book away and turn on the television. By contrast, well-arranged paragraphs make a book or article look inviting.

Secondly and perhaps more importantly, paragraphs provide a way for a writer to organize his or her thoughts. Ideally, each new paragraph should be a signal that the author is about to develop a new idea or change direction in some way. Thus, paragraphs help readers to keep track of the author's different points without getting confused.

How long should a paragraph be? For most purposes, the best answer is "Neither too long nor too short." A paragraph that goes on for more than a page is long enough to scare or confuse most readers. On the other hand, a series of very short paragraphs will give the impression that the writer is neither thinking clearly nor organizing carefully. For a beginning writer, five or six sentences is probably a good length for a typical paragraph.

Short paragraphs sometimes have their uses, however. We have already seen that in a conversation, a new paragraph begins with each change of speaker—even if the result is a paragraph that is only one word long, for example:

"Delbert, what have you been doing all day?" Coach Wilson asked. "Isn't there something you want to tell me?"

"No."

"Let's be honest, Delbert. I know you skipped classes and went to Dead Man's Pond this morning."

You can emphasize an important sentence by giving it a paragraph of its own. Like any device used for emphasis, this trick should be saved for rare and special occasions.

As a beginning writer, you may find it useful to practice the **topic sentence,** which usually appears early in a paragraph (the first or second sentence) and indicates what the subject is to be.

For example, a paragraph might begin with this statement: "Every student should learn to play a musical instrument." In the

Writing Tip: If you are writing for a newspaper, your paragraphs will be short—only two or three sentences—because the narrow columns will make any paragraph look longer than it really is.

sentences that follow, the writer would list reasons for including music in every school curriculum. Occasionally, however, a writer will reverse this method and postpone the topic sentence until the end of the paragraph.

> *A student who can play a trumpet or a clarinet will find endless opportunities to have fun and make friends. She can strut proudly in the homecoming parade, play in the community orchestra's Mozart festival, or shine in the Red-Hot Radio Talent Contest. Traveling with a school band will teach her to get along and work together with a busload of rowdy or carsick classmates. She can put on a lacy dress and play a solo at her best friend's formal wedding, or she can wear a purple blazer and perform with a jazz combo. She might even earn enough money later to buy textbooks and paper through a college scholarship. More importantly, performing such music as Beethoven's "Ode to Joy" will develop her sensitivity and teach her to enjoy life. Every student should learn to play a musical instrument.*

As you expand upon your topic sentence, try to be as specific as possible. For example, suppose you begin with this topic sentence: *"The dog deserves his reputation as man's best friend."* To complete the paragraph, you will need more than a few vague restatements of the topic.

> **Poor:** *The dog deserves his reputation as man's best friend. Throughout history, the dog has been a faithful and loyal companion to humankind. Humans never feel alone when their trusty dogs are at their side. A dog is one friend that a human can always count on.*

All of these statements may be true, but they give us little information about the value of dogs. You need to give specific examples: dogs can be trained to see for the blind and care for the severely disabled; dogs are invaluable on the farm and in police cars; dogs are protectors of children and companions for the elderly; dogs like Lassie and Rin Tin Tin have even become famous as movie and television stars; and nothing can ease sorrow or disappointment like the caress of a moist tongue and the soft touch of a furry head in one's lap.

> **Writing Tip:** When writing a report, make sure all the sentences in a paragraph support the topic sentence.

Such methods work well for nonfiction, but when a writer is telling a story, his topic sentences will probably be less obvious. Instead of stating the subject of the paragraph, an opening sentence may simply indicate some change in the action, as in:

> *Feeling tired and hungry, Kevin left the shack and started toward home. He walked with dragging feet as he thought over the events of the day. Such a waste of time and energy! He and Laurie had nothing to show for their efforts except aching muscles and an unreadable map. And time was growing short: they had only three days until the next full moon.*
>
> *Then, as Kevin walked past the old water tower, he saw something that brought a chill to his spine. . . .*

Name: _____   Date: _____

ASSIGNMENT: Practicing the Paragraph

Develop each of the following topic sentences into a good paragraph:

1. My hometown is an interesting (or boring) place to live.

    _____

    _____

    _____

    _____

    _____

    _____

    _____

2. Grades should be abolished in American schools.

    _____

    _____

    _____

    _____

    _____

    _____

    _____

3. Physical fitness is important for everyone.

    _____

    _____

    _____

    _____

    _____

    _____

    _____

BRAINWORK: *Write a good paragraph on a topic of your choice. Make certain that your paragraph has a topic sentence. You may place the topic sentence either at the beginning or the end of your paragraph.*

PART SIX: WRITING PROSE

30. Style

Style is the quality that makes a composition easy to understand and pleasant to read. Style is a different matter from grammar. In the study of grammar, we use such terms as *right* and *wrong, good* and *bad, correct* and *incorrect.* Style, however, is more complicated. One could write a perfectly "correct" composition using nothing except passive verbs, but because passive verbs are less interesting than active ones, such a composition would show poor style.

Developing a good style takes time and practice. There is no perfect set of rules for style, but there are some useful guidelines. We have already looked at a few of them: use active verbs whenever you can, avoid dangling and misplaced modifiers, use different types and lengths of sentences, avoid split constructions, use specific examples, stick to one tense as much as possible, pay attention to paragraphs. Below are a few more things to remember.

Save the most interesting or important words for the end of the sentence. Here is an example of poor style:

> *When I walked into the hallway and tripped over a corpse, it was three o'clock in the afternoon.*

For most people, tripping over a corpse would be more interesting—or at least more memorable—than looking at a clock and noticing that the time was 3:00 P.M. Unless the hour is an essential clue to solving a murder mystery, it would be better to write the sentence in this way: *At three o'clock in the afternoon I walked into the hallway and tripped over a corpse.* This same advice applies to writing a paragraph: Save your most interesting sentence until the end.

Use parallel structure. In other words, state similar ideas in similar grammatical form.

> **Writing Tip:** Good writing style develops through practice, not through memorizing rules. The more you practice, the better your style gets!

> **Poor style:** *The dog barked, and an answering howl was heard from the werewolf.* (No logical reason for the shift from an intransitive verb to a passive verb.)
> **Better:** *The dog barked, and the werewolf howled in reply.*

In a series, every item should be grammatically similar. That is, you may write a series of nouns, a series of verbs, a series of prepositional phrases, any kind of series—but not a series that consists of two adjectives, a prepositional phrase, and a verb.

Poor: *Jack Shmoot was handsome, friendly, with a lot of talent at baseball, and had many fans.*

Better: *Jack Shmoot, the famous baseball player, was handsome, friendly, talented, and popular.* (series of adjectives)

Parallel structure is a favorite device of poets, orators, and preachers. Here are some famous examples:

Ask not what your country can do for you; ask what you can do for your country. (from John F. Kennedy's inaugural address)

Love never fails; but whether there be prophecies, they shall fail; whether there be tongues, they shall cease; whether there be knowledge, it shall vanish away. (from the Bible)

I came; I saw; I conquered. (Julius Caesar)

Avoid careless repetition of a word. This rule can be difficult to apply. If you are writing about dogs, you will have to use the word *dog* a good many times. Repetition as part of parallel structure can be effective and even beautiful. But avoid sentences like this one:

The big black dog continued to dog my footsteps doggedly all through the dog days of August.

You may find you make many of these mistakes when you write a first draft. Do not despair! All writers—novelists, journalists, poets, business people, and more—take the time to read what they wrote and catch mistakes like these. Revising your writing to edit for style is a skill that is almost as valuable as writing itself. Not only will your writing improve, but as you write and revise, you will soon find you make fewer mistakes in your first drafts.

> **Writing Tip:** Remember, all writers have different styles, and each person's style develops over time.

Name: _____ Date: _____

ASSIGNMENT: Style

Rewrite each of the following sentences to improve the style:

1. I learned that I had won a million dollars in the state lottery while washing the dishes.

    _____

    _____

2. I hate baked beans, but they are loved by most of my friends.

    _____

    _____

3. To succeed at archery, an athlete must be calm, healthy, independent, and have great patience. _____

    _____

4. Watching from the back porch, the sunset was an inspiring sight.

    _____

    _____

5. The alarm was heard by the firemen, and the gleaming red truck was driven by them to the burning school. _____

    _____

6. When I confessed to the principal that I had accidentally set the school on fire, it was early the next morning. _____

    _____

7. I have ever since I was five years old and just starting kindergarten dreamed of becoming an astronaut. _____

    _____

8. Detective Trilby made a complete investigation, and the solution to the mystery was discovered by her. _____

    _____

Writing Prompt: *Write a paragraph beginning with this topic sentence:* Freedom is important to every American. *Use parallel structure wherever you can.*

PART SIX: WRITING PROSE

31. What Is an Essay?

An **essay** is a short work of nonfiction. The difference between an essay and an article is that an article deals mainly with facts, but an essay is more concerned with thoughts, opinions, emotions, and moods.

The essay was invented during the sixteenth century by the French writer Montaigne. The English word *essay* comes from the French word *essai,* which means "attempt." When Montaigne created the essay, he was interested in writing about his own thoughts and interests; he had no fondness for rigid rules. So, as one might expect, an essayist has a great deal of freedom. An essay can be humorous, sad, inspiring, bitter, or deeply serious. An essay might be only four hundred words long—less than two double-spaced typewritten pages—or it may be thirty pages of fine print. An essayist can protest against injustice, pose solutions to the problems of the world, or simply laugh at the small problems of everyday life. The title of an essay could be anything from "My Thoughts About Mosquitoes" to "Let's Have World Peace, Now."

Essays have changed the world. In the 1770s, Thomas Paine wrote essays that inspired the American colonists to fight for their freedom from England. After the American Revolution, Alexander Hamilton and James Madison wrote the *Federalist* essays, which convinced Americans to accept the new Constitution and create the United States as we know it. In the next century, Henry David Thoreau protested slavery by refusing to pay a small tax. As a result, he spent a night in jail and later wrote an essay about his experience. That essay, which is known by the title "Civil Disobedience," has encouraged protesters around the world to peacefully advance their causes. Mahatma Gandhi used Thoreau's ideas when he led the struggle for India's independence from England. Later Thoreau's essay inspired Martin Luther King, Jr., leader of the American civil-rights movement.

Because most modern essays are short, the essay is a favorite with busy readers who do not have time to wade through long books. Today, newspapers and magazines are filled with essays on every imaginable subject. Because of their brevity, essays also make good writing assignments for students in schools. A typical student essay is 250–500 words in length—one or two typewritten pages, or two or three handwritten pages.

Writing Tip: The student essay may also be called a **theme,** a **composition,** or simply a **paper.**

The essay has no unbreakable rules, but over the years, writers and teachers have developed a few useful guidelines. We will study some of these in the next few chapters. For the beginner, it is a good idea to keep an essay short—four or five paragraphs is a good length—and to plan each paragraph carefully.

Critical Thinking: Can you think of any good reasons why a rebellious person like Thoreau would find it appealing to write essays? Explain your answer.

PART SIX: WRITING PROSE

32. The Good Old Reliable Three-Point Essay

Does your mind go blank when you have to prepare a speech for civics class or write an English assignment? Do you stare at your notebook, chew your pen, and ask yourself helplessly, "What can I write about?" or "What can I say?" If so, there is an easy solution to your problem. All you have to do is pick a topic—any topic—and say three things about it. Give three examples of leadership, three reasons why your school should abolish grades, three results of poor study habits, or three things you hate about worms. Such an essay is called a **three-point enumeration.**

The three-point essay is short, easy to organize, easy to prepare, and easy for a reader or listener to remember. The best way to organize a three-point essay is to plan five paragraphs. In the first paragraph, you should introduce your subject and indicate what your approach will be to your three points. A good introduction captures the reader's attention and makes him want to read further. Avoid boring introductions such as "In this paper I will try to explain three results of poor study habits." Instead, you might begin like this:

Brrrrring! The alarm clock sounds in my ear. Another Monday morning has arrived, and I never opened a book all weekend. What if Mr. Johnson gives another one of his diabolical pop tests today? Suddenly I feel too sick to eat breakfast. My poor study habits are giving me nervous indigestion, ruining my self-confidence, and destroying my hopes for a college scholarship.

The next three paragraphs should cover the three main points: a paragraph about indigestion, a paragraph about self-confidence, a final and perhaps longer paragraph about college and scholarships. Be sure to save your most important or most interesting point until the fourth paragraph. Your fifth paragraph should be a conclusion in which you summarize or perhaps suggest some kind of action.

> **Writing Tip:** In a five-paragraph essay, be sure to save your most important point for the fourth paragraph.

But I refuse to give up. I'm tired of being sick at my stomach, tired of feeling guilty, tired of worrying about college. Starting today, I'm going to use the study hall and the library for studying instead of daydreaming. Starting tonight, I'll finish my homework before I watch television. University of Chicago, here I come!

There is no magic in the number three, but a good writer or speaker will be wary of boring or confusing his readers or audience. "I want to say three things about freedom," the Mayor says at a campaign rally. He might also say five things about freedom and still keep everyone's attention. But if he says seven things, he's in trouble, and if he says 29 things, his speech will be a disaster. Half of the audience will be snickering, the other half will be grinding their teeth, and no one will remember anything about freedom.

Name: _____   Date: _____

ASSIGNMENT: Planning the Three-point Enumeration Essay

1. Think of a change that you believe should be made in your school, your city, your state, or the country.

   _____

   _____

   List three reasons why this change would be a good idea.

   a. _____

   b. _____

   c. _____

   Think of a good title for your essay:

   _____

Essay: *On your own paper, write a three-point essay about your proposed change. Put your title at the top of the first page.*

2. Think of a favorite place—a town, city, vacation spot, building, beach, or any place where you like to spend time.

   _____

   _____

   List three reasons why this place is your favorite:

   a. _____

   b. _____

   c. _____

   Think of a good title for your essay:

   _____

Essay: *On your own paper, write a three-point essay about your favorite place. Put your title at the top of the first page.*

PART SIX: WRITING PROSE

33. How to Get Rich Quick! The Process Essay

Whether we will admit it or not, most of us are confused most of the time. Life is filled with perplexing questions: What is that funny smell in the basement? Why is my computer making a noise like a broken foghorn? Should I save my money or spend it on a new pair of running shoes? What would Darcy say if I asked her to go with me to the seventh-grade dance? What would happen if I pushed the green button on the wall next to the fire extinguisher—the one marked *For Emergencies Only*?

In short, most of us need all the advice we can get, and a writer who has good advice to give will always find an eager response. Browse through a newspaper, a magazine rack, or a bookstore and notice the titles: "How to Save Your Money and Become a Millionaire Before Your Twenty-Fifth Birthday!"; "How to Improve Your Love Life"; *Common Emergencies and How to Cope with Them.* The **process essay** and the **how-to-do-it** article and book are favorites with readers everywhere.

Do you have any advice to give? You probably don't have the key to instant wealth, but probably you do have some area of special knowledge—how to perfect the slam-dunk, become a competent babysitter, earn a merit badge in Scouting, care for a pet, or play the piano. You could write a process essay that people would find useful.

There are some important things to remember about process essays. First, it is correct to use the second person viewpoint *(you, yours,* and *your)* and imperative sentences. In many types of writing, the words *you, yours,* and *your* are either irritating or completely out of place, and a teacher often objects to these words when they appear in student papers. But the second person viewpoint is perfectly natural in a how-to-do-it piece. After all, the essay is addressed directly to the reader, who is a second person.

Second, a process essay needs to be clear and well organized. Never forget that your reader is *ignorant.* After all, if he already knew how to care for a pet or make oyster stew, he wouldn't be reading your essay. He is depending on you for instructions, so make certain that you don't leave out any important steps. For example, tell your reader to drain the canned oysters before adding them to the stew. This simple step may seem so obvious that you will be tempted to skip it and save paper, but remember: *Your reader is ignorant.* If you don't tell him to drain the can of oysters, he will probably wind up with oyster soup instead of oyster stew.

To avoid giving bad or incomplete advice, you should make a list of the important steps before you write your paper. List them in order, and check to see if you left anything out. Then, when you write your paper, be as clear and specific as you can. And remember that a process essay doesn't have to be solemn or serious; it can also be light-hearted or amusing. For example, you might write an essay entitled "How to Become a First-Rate Nuisance" or "The Fine Art of Wasting Time."

Writing Tip: Process essays are also called *how-to essays*.

Name: _____ Date: _____

ASSIGNMENT: Planning the Process Essay

Write a list of things that you know how to do:

_____

_____

_____

_____

_____

Choose the one that would be most interesting to read about.

_____

List the steps in performing this process. Be sure to list them in order. Use extra paper if necessary.

1. _____

2. _____

3. _____

4. _____

5. _____

6. _____

7. _____

8. _____

9. _____

Think of a good title for your essay:

_____

Essay: *On your own paper, develop your list of steps into a good process essay. Try to give your paper an eye-catching introduction and a strong conclusion. Aim at four or five paragraphs, and place your title at the top of the first page.*

PART SIX: WRITING PROSE

34. Comparing and Contrasting

To **compare** means to point out similarities; to **contrast** means to point out differences. Both comparing and contrasting help people to understand their problems and find solutions to those problems. For example, if your soccer team has lost every game so far, your coach might help break the losing streak by contrasting your team with the Quincy Panthers, who are ranked first in the state. What exactly are the Panthers doing that your team is not? Holding longer practice sessions? Holding shorter but more frequent sessions? Getting more sleep and rest? Such a *contrast* might provide ideas that would help your soccer team improve its record, or at least help you plan for next season.

Either comparison or contrast can serve as the basis of an interesting essay. In either case, the trick to writing a good essay is the choice of subject. To write a good comparison, you must choose two subjects that are different in some important ways; otherwise your essay will be pointless. It would be a boring exercise, for example, to compare the physical characteristics of a pair of identical twins. (Susan has blue eyes; Sarah also has blue eyes. Susan is five feet tall; Sarah is also five feet tall. . . .) But it might be interesting to compare two sisters who look as different as the sun and the moon but who have similar personalities. Likewise, in order for a contrast to be meaningful, the two subjects must be similar in many ways. It would be pointless to contrast a raisin with the Washington Monument, but it might be instructive to contrast two soccer teams or two politicians.

35. The Personal Essay

To write a **personal essay** is to write about yourself—your experiences, thoughts, moods, dreams, fears, likes, and dislikes. Such an assignment is less conceited than it sounds, because in a personal essay you will be introducing yourself to a reader just as you introduce yourself to a stranger who might become a friend.

The personal essay has no rigid rules, but you have your choice of a number of approaches. You might tell a story about a memorable adventure or mishap that you once experienced. (This approach is called **narration.**) Or you might describe a person who is dear to you or a place about which you feel strong emotions. You can write about problems—serious problems, like the plight of the homeless, or trivial annoyances, like the bullet-proof pancakes at Bob's Diner. You can write about how you react to an everyday situation of life: waiting in line, getting ready for a dance, failing a test, walking through the city streets, looking at the stars on a moonlit night, listening to rain on the roof.

The goal of the personal essay is for the author to present himself or herself as a likable or interesting person, so try not to sound self-centered. Instead, give the impression that you are aware of and interested in the world around you. You may use the words "I," "me," "my," and "mine," but not in every sentence.

ANSWER KEYS

Note: Many of the activities are open-ended. Only activities with definite answers are listed here.

Working With Pronouns (page 8)

1. Joe ran into the gymnasium and found (it) empty. "Kristin! Coach Wilson!" (he) shouted. "Miss Peterson! (Anybody)! Can (you) hear (me)?" But (no one) answered. Joe's shout echoed eerily among the shadows of the gymnasium. (He) looked in the locker room; (it) was also empty, and the door to Coach Wilson's office was locked. Apparently (everyone) had left for the day. "(This) is spooky," Joe said aloud. (He) always felt braver when (he) talked to (himself).

   Joe whistled to keep (his) courage strong as (he) tried to think of a plan. Then (he) remembered: sometimes Kristin went to the library to read, so maybe Joe would find (her) there. "(That's) a good idea," (he) said as (he) hurried back to the parking lot. "Next stop—the public library!" Suddenly (he) stopped and stared in disbelief. (His) bicycle was gone! (Someone), or (something), had taken (it). "*Now* what do (I) do?" (he) said in a shaking voice. (He) could never reach the library on foot—not before sunset. Sherlock Holmes (himself) couldn't find a way out of such a mess.

Parts of Speech (page 19)

1. verb	6. preposition	11. noun
2. conjunction	7. adverb	12. conjunction
3. interjection	8. adverb	13. article (adj.)
4. adjective	9. verb	14. verb
5. noun	10. adjective	15. adverb

Verbals (page 30)

1. participle	8. gerund	15. gerund
2. infinitive	9. infinitive	16. infinitive
3. gerund	10. participle	17. participle
4. infinitive	11. infinitive	18. gerund
5. participle	12. participle	19. infinitive
6. participle	13. infinitive	20. gerund
7. participle	14. infinitive	

Types of Phrases (page 33)

1. infinitive phrase	11. infinitive phrase
2. gerund phrase	12. infinitive phrase
3. infinitive phrase	13. gerund phrase
4. prepositional phrase	14. verb phrase
5. verb phrase	15. prepositional phrase
6. gerund phrase	16. infinitive phrase
7. infinitive phrase	17. prepositional phrase
8. prepositional phrase	18. infinitive phrase
9. participle phrase	19. prepositional phrase
10. infinitive phrase	20. prepositional phrase

Types of Sentences (page 36)

1. declarative	6. imperative	11. declarative
2. imperative	7. declarative	12. interrogative
3. interrogative	8. interrogative	13. interrogative
4. declarative	9. declarative	14. interrogative
5. exclamatory	10. exclamatory	15. imperative

Restrictive & Non-Restrictive Clauses (page 45)

1. Laurie showed the strange map to her mother, who was a librarian.
2. C
3. C
4. Any book that was borrowed from Madison Library had to be returned in three weeks.
5. C
6. C
7. Kevin decided to call his oldest brother, who was a computer specialist.
8. Summer Cove, which was Kevin's hometown, was a place where there were many legends about pirates.
9. C
10. C
11. When the Chief of Police, a man named Bob Brugger, got the lab results back, he gave them to his top detective, Sue Jamison.
12. C
13. She also began taking fingerprints, which was standard procedure.
14. Then the police department, which is located downtown, received an anonymous tip.
15. The thief was Timothy Barden, who owned the local gift store, Pirate's Cove.

Using Commas (page 51)

1. Scott wanted to act in the school play, but he had a soft voice.
2. When he got up on the stage and read for the part of Ebeneezer Scrooge, no one in the back rows could understand his words.
3. Ebeneezer Scrooge has to speak in a loud, gruff voice.
4. If an actor wants to be convincing as Ebeneezer Scrooge, he must be forceful, imaginative, and dramatic.
5. Some people, of course, have little talent for acting.
6. Feeling disappointed because of his failure to win even a small part in *A Christmas Carol,* Scott went home, heaved a sigh, and collapsed in front of the television set.
7. Scott's mother, who was an electrician, told him to try out for the lighting crew.
8. *A Christmas Carol,* which is based on a book by Charles Dickens, requires a lot of special lighting effects.
9. Scott knew all about electrical wiring, so the director appointed him head of the lighting crew.
10. Scott, who was very creative, made an excellent addition to the crew, and he was often asked to solve some of the most difficult lighting problems.

ANSWER KEYS

11. *A Christmas Carol* was a big success, and when Scott didn't get a part in the next play, he wasn't very disappointed.
12. He remained head of the lighting crew for the entire school year.
13. Even though he did not appear in a single play, Scott was chosen as the Outstanding Theatre Student of the year.
14. Everyone loved his work, and he decided that next year he would remain head of the lighting crew and only take small parts if he was needed instead of hoping for a major part in a play and not getting to work with the lighting.

Working With Punctuation Marks (page 54)

Dear Mr. Sterling Noble:

Last night I read in the newspaper that you are planning to direct a major motion picture entitled *Hercules: The Strongest Man in History*. I am qualified to play Hercules for the following reasons: my strength, my acting ability, and my handsome face.

Everyone who knows me agrees that I am strong. I get up at 4:00 every morning to jog and lift weights. I follow my exercise period with a big breakfast of bran muffins, fat-free sausage, low-calorie pancakes, wheat cereal, and skim milk. I pick up every heavy object in sight. People are always asking me to carry groceries and move furniture for them.

I am also a good actor. When I was a tiny baby only two days old, I played the role of the Baby New Year in a church pageant, and I have been acting ever since. I can play heroes, villains, and ordinary people. I have played a tree in *The Wizard of Oz,* a windmill in *Don Quixote,* and a clock in *Cinderella*. As for my face, you can see that I am handsome; all you have to do is look at the enclosed photograph. Everyone tells me that I am the handsomest young man in Little, Illinois, which is my hometown. I know you'll agree, Mr. Noble, that you need me to play Hercules. When can I come to Hollywood for an audition?

Sincerely yours,

Buffalo Brutus

The Apostrophe & Other Punctuation (page 60)

1. Don't tell me about your problems, because I'm tired of listening.
2. The police can't find out who's responsible for stealing Coach Wilson's wallet.
3. Beth's kitten has hurt its paw, so we'll take it to the veterinarian's clinic.
4. John, haven't you finished feeding the horses yet?

5. Let's borrow Amy's bicycle, go to the store, and buy cookies, popcorn, and candy.
6. The women's basketball team has won all of their games this season.
7. Can't you figure out what the problem is?
8. C
9. They're going to raise the price of football tickets this season; now, they're going to cost a fortune!
10. Look, Leslie, it's not going to happen, so stop asking about it!
11. Whose bike is parked in the middle of the living room?
12. C
13. C
14. Harry told me to—wait, don't you want to know what he said?
15. I can't believe I forgot to study for the test: now I'm going to fail!
16. My mom's so mean, she won't buy me that new game system.
17. C
18. I won't be at the basketball game tonight, because I've got to go visit my grandmother.
19. The princess's (or princess') gown was long, blue, and covered with tiny pearls.
20. I don't just believe in ghosts—I've <u>seen</u> one.

Punctuation (page 66)

1. Detective Trilby asked the band leader whether he had ever seen an evil wizard in the castle.
2. Detective Trilby, a clever woman, said to the king, "I know who's responsible for the evil spells."
3. The fish pond and the moat were overflowing, and the faucets were pouring water into the castle.
4. Darcy Andrews lived in Little, Illinois, but her dream was to work for NASA.
5. "Miss Andrews," said the teacher, "come down from outer space and stop dreaming about satellites and rockets."
6. Darcy lived across the street from Mr. Porter's neighborhood grocery store.
7. Mr. Porter, who believed in flying saucers, gave some of his old science fiction magazines to Darcy.
8. One bright day in October, Darcy went to the store to buy a loaf of bread and found Mr. Porter hiding under the counter.
9. "Hide quick!" he whispered to Darcy. "I just saw an alien from outer space."
10. "Are you sure it wasn't a child in a Halloween costume?" Darcy asked.

Sentence Fragments (page 68)

1. I plan to go to the Singing Zombies concert if I can convince Mom to buy me a ticket.

ANSWER KEYS

2. Correct
3. Correct
4. Jason is a good actor who practices in front of a mirror until he can speak his lines perfectly.
5. Alice searched all morning and afternoon but couldn't find the lost puppy.
6. Correct, but if you don't want to start a sentence with a conjunction you could change it to: Alice was starting to grow discouraged, but she refused to give up.
7. Darcy wandered through the dark woods, growing more frightened every minute.
8. This week our soccer team plays the Quincy Panthers, a team that is almost impossible to beat.
9. The Panthers' mascot is Norbert Swizzle, who dresses like a giant black cat and dances the Charleston while twirling a baton.
10. Correct

Sentence Fragments, Comma Splices, and Run-On Sentences (page 70)

Answers will vary; possible answers include.
1. Eric's house has an unusual feature. There is a secret room behind the fireplace.
2. Eric and his friends have a clubhouse in the secret room, where they like to meet and play a board game called *Sword and Sorcery.*
3. Sometimes they also play chess and checkers or hold business meetings and elections.
4. Correct
5. Correct, but if you want to avoid beginning a sentence with a conjunction: The secret room has no electricity, but the members use candles to light their meetings.
6. Eric's house is surrounded by a stone wall and big trees, which make the place look dark and mysterious.
7. Correct
8. The secret room is a mystery because nobody knows why it was built into the house.
9. None of the family diaries or other records say anything about a secret room. Eric's great-grandmother can't explain the mystery either.
10. All the family knows is that the room has been a family secret. The room wasn't even shown to the electrician who installed the electricity in the house many years ago.

Subject-Verb Agreement (page 73)

1. Jerry and Beth are working together on a school project.
2. They have organized an election for president of Mrs. Andrews' government class.
3. Correct
4. Correct

5. Two political parties have been formed by the class, and everyone has chosen a party to join.
6. Correct
7. Gerry Davies was chosen by the other party as their nominee.
8. Correct
9. Mrs. Andrews or two students present the latest election news every day before class starts.
10. Davies and Taylor were in a close race, but Taylor won.

Dangling and Misplaced Modifiers (page 75)

Answers will vary; possible answers include.
1. While I was walking down the dusty road, a black convertible roared over the hill and almost struck me.
2. As she was sleeping peacefully, the alarm clock rang in Jenny's ear.
3. After eating a big Sunday dinner, I thought a nap seemed like a good idea.
4. Stumbling sleepily into the classroom, Delbert dropped his books to the floor.
5. The audience in the balcony cheered when Tonya finished her piano solo.
6. Serious automobile accidents can occur when drivers travel on icy roads.
7. People who are superstitious often avoid black cats.
8. While nibbling popcorn and watching television, I saw Biff Williams run eighty yards for a touchdown.
9. After skating perfectly, my brother won a gold medal at the State Winter Olympics.
10. Mother made a cake that was dripping with chocolate frosting for the family.

Style (page 85)

Answers will vary; possible answers include the following.
1. While washing the dishes, I learned that I had won a million dollars in the state lottery.
2. I hate baked beans, but most of my friends love them.
3. To succeed at archery, an athlete must be calm, healthy, independent, and patient.
4. I watched the inspiring sunset from the back porch.
5. The firemen heard the alarm and drove the gleaming red truck to the burning school.
6. Early the next morning, I confessed to the principal that I had accidentally set the school on fire.
7. Ever since I was five years old and just starting kindergarten, I have dreamed of becoming an astronaut.
8. Detective Trilby made a complete investigation and discovered the solution to the mystery.